KINGDOM
MEN
RISING

KINGDOM MEN RISING

A CALL TO GROWTH AND GREATER INFLUENCE

TONY EVANS

BETHANYHOUSE
a division of Baker Publishing Group
Minneapolis, Minnesota

© 2021 by Dr. Tony Evans

Published by Bethany House Publishers
11400 Hampshire Avenue South
Bloomington, Minnesota 55438
www.bethanyhouse.com

Bethany House Publishers is a division of
Baker Publishing Group, Grand Rapids, Michigan

Printed in the United States of America

Library of Congress Cataloging-in-Publication Data
Names: Evans, Tony, author.
Title: Kingdom men rising : a call to growth and greater influence / Tony Evans.
Description: Minneapolis, Minnesota : Bethany House, a division of Baker Publishing Group, 2021. | Includes bibliographical references.
Identifiers: LCCN 2020046867 | ISBN 9780764237058 (cloth) | ISBN 9780764237065 (trade paperback) | ISBN 9781493430116 (ebook)
Subjects: LCSH: Christian men—Religious life. | Spiritual formation. | Discipling (Christianity)
Classification: LCC BV4528.2 .E918 2021 | DDC 248.8/42—dc23
LC record available at https://lccn.loc.gov/2020046867

Some material in chapter 2 adapted from Tony Evans, *America: Turning a Nation to God* (Chicago: Moody, 2015), chapter 2.

Portions of chapter 6 adapted from *30 Days to Overcoming Addictive Behavior*, Copyright © 2017 Tony Evans. Published by Harvest House Publishers, Eugene, Oregon 97408. www.harvesthouse publishers.com

Other material in chapter 6 adapted from *It's Not Too Late*, Copyright © 2012 Tony Evans. Published by Harvest House Publishers, Eugene, Oregon 97408. www.harvesthousepublishers.com

A segment of chapter 8 adapted from Tony Evans, *Oneness Embraced* (Chicago: Moody, 2015), chapter 2.

Some material in chapter 12 adapted from Tony Evans, *Raising Kingdom Kids: Giving Your Child a Living Faith* (Carol Stream, IL: Focus on the Family book published by Tyndale, 2014), chapter 11.

Cover design by Dan Pitts

21 22 23 24 25 26 27   7 6 5 4 3 2 1

CONTENTS

Dedication   7

Acknowledgments   9

Introduction   11

PART ONE: AWAKENING BIBLICAL MANHOOD   13

1. Chosen for the Challenge   15
2. Dry Bones Can Dance   33
3. A Tale of Two Men   47
4. The Secret to Success   61

PART TWO: UNLEASHING BIBLICAL MANHOOD   83

5. Get Up   85
6. Get Over   99
7. Get Going   117
8. Get Along   135

PART THREE: TRANSFERRING BIBLICAL MANHOOD   155

9. Setting the Stage   157
10. Furthering the Future   179

11. Identifying Key Influencers   195

12. Starting the Transfer   211

   Appendix A: Kingdom Declaration   225
   Appendix B: The Urban Alternative   227
   Notes   235
   About the Author   239

This book is dedicated to my sons-in-law, Jerry Shirer and Jessie Hurst, who continue the process of messaging and modeling the principles of *Kingdom Men Rising* to my daughters, grandchildren, and great-grandchildren.

ACKNOWLEDGMENTS

I want to thank my friends at Baker Publishing Group for their interest and partnership in bringing my thoughts, study, and words to print on this valuable subject. I particularly want to thank Andy McGuire for leading the charge on this manuscript with Baker Publishing Group. It's been a pleasure working with Andy to see this through to print. I also want to publicly thank Sharon Hodge and Hannah Ahlfield. In addition, my appreciation goes out to Heather Hair for her skills and insights in writing and collaboration on not only this manuscript, but also on my book *Kingdom Man*.

INTRODUCTION

When you purchase a game of checkers, you'll notice that on the top of each piece is the insignia of a crown. That is because each checker was created to become a king.

Once it is crowned because it has successfully made it to the other side of the board, it will have the right and authority to maneuver and function at a much higher level than it could prior to being crowned. The reality is, however, that most individual checkers will not successfully make it to the other end of the board to be crowned, because the opposition will jump them and knock them out of the game. Whether a checker achieves its created goal of being crowned as a king is fully determined by the moves that are made underneath the hand of the one controlling it.

When God created men, He created them with a crown because each man was made to rule under the authority of God. God created the man prior to creating the woman, like pouring a foundation first, because the success or failure of God's created purpose of building His kingdom in history would be directly related to a man's relationship with and submission to God's rule over his life. Foundations don't have to be fancy or pretty, but they do have to be strong. When a foundation is weak, everything resting on it is at risk. God holds the man ultimately responsible for keeping steady what He has entrusted to his care while simultaneously advancing His kingdom program.

However, as with the first man, Adam, Satan is seeking to "jump" men to keep us from fulfilling our divinely ordained kingdom purposes. He goes to great lengths to remove us from functioning in alignment with God so that our families, churches, communities, and nation experience the negative consequences and confusion of men living independently of God.

It is evident that our spiritual energy has kept too many men in a cycle of defeat, discouragement, confusion, rebellion, addiction, and a myriad of other things that have resulted in the spiritual, social, racial, and political chaos we are experiencing today. Far too many men have become either neutered and domesticated or abusive and irresponsible, resulting in a society that is torn, tattered, and in utter dysfunction.

Yet, despite all we see around us, there remains hope. If God can get His men to rise up as the kingdom men He has created us to be—men who pursue an intimate relationship with Him while simultaneously representing Him in all we do—He will reverse the downward spiral of the culture. God is waiting on His kingdom men to rise from our spiritual slumber to accept the responsibility of reversing the decay and disunity that engulf us.

Just as the first Adam brought defeat to the human race, the last Adam, Jesus Christ, came to bring victory. It's time for God's men, under the lordship of Jesus Christ, to change the trajectory of our culture as we submit ourselves to Him and His kingdom agenda.

It is my goal, in *Kingdom Men Rising*, to challenge you and all of us as men to accept and implement the responsibility handed to us by our Creator. This responsibility involves not only rising to the challenges we face but also influencing a whole generation of men and boys to do the same. If God's kingdom men decide to rise up to fulfill our calling, we can see Him heal our hearts, our families, our churches, and our land.

It's time to join a new movement of men who long to see what God will do with the awakening of His kingdom men who lead their families and infiltrate the culture as kingdom citizens. Men who proudly and victoriously wear our crowns and are used by God to crown the next generation with kingdom values.

Dr. Tony Evans
Dallas, Texas

PART ONE

AWAKENING BIBLICAL MANHOOD

ONE

CHOSEN FOR THE CHALLENGE

"A kingdom man is the kind of man that when his feet hit the floor each morning the devil says, 'Oh crap, he's up!'"

When I first wrote that line to open my book *Kingdom Man* nearly ten years ago, I had no idea how deeply I would be put to the test in living it out. But on New Year's Eve 2019, I was scheduled to preach like I always do to usher in the New Year. But this night was unlike past New Year's Eves.

Typically, these services ring loudly with cheer, great music, laughter, and fun. We hold two services so that thousands upon thousands can come. We always end the second service with a countdown to the New Year right at midnight. But this night was different. This night stared me straight in the face, daring me to stay down.

I had lain in my bed for the better part of that entire day, as well as the previous one. All lights had been turned out, curtains were closed, and I had pulled the covers up to my chin. My empty stare reflected the empty ache inside.

From time to time, one of the kids would come into the room to check on me and see if I needed anything to eat or drink. I did not. They asked me if I had gotten any sleep. I had not. They reminded me that I needed to try. I disagreed. Because all I needed right then was my wife.

But Lois had gone on to be with the Lord just the morning before. She'd asked me to let her go weeks earlier, since she could tell her time had come, and I had sat by her bed weeping as I told her I could not. But a few more weeks of witnessing her suffer through the effects of the cancer that ravaged her once-vibrant life brought me to my knees. I relented. I surrendered. I told my bride of forty-nine and a half years I would let her go this time.

I told her she could go now and be with her parents, whom, in this final stage of her transition, she had seen appear in our room from time to time. I told her she could go be with Jesus, whom she loved so much that she had asked us to write His name down just because it made her happy to see it. I told her she could go get the award that the angels, she had found the strength to tell us, had said she was about to receive. "An award, an award," she said a few days before she died. "They are going to give me an award." Lois was ready, even if I was not.

I took comfort, though, knowing that she had been shown tremendous love and had taken great joy in our family surrounding her throughout her final months on earth. She had never been left alone. By and large, my work schedule had come to a near halt for the bulk of an entire year so that I could be there with her every step of the way. Each treatment. Each doctor visit. Each new meal of health-promising potential. Each prayer. Each day. Each tear. She had become my sole focus. She had become our sole focus as a family. But now, here I was, alone in a room I had shared with my best friend for decades. What's more, I was scheduled to go preach.

Yet how could I even get up?

I knew that everyone would understand if I decided not to preach that night. No one would blame me for staying home to grieve. No one except Lois. Her faith in God propelled all that she did throughout our life together. I knew she'd want me there. In fact, earlier that year—on the very night we had gathered our four kids around us to tell them of the return of her cancer—she had reminded us all how to face this challenge.

This painful blow came the very same night I received the prestigious National Religious Broadcasters Hall of Fame Award. Our kids had flown with us to Los Angeles to witness me receive it. But now, only hours after the honor, we sat in a hotel room crying as a family.

After allowing each of us a moment to express our emotions at the telling of the doctors' news, Lois called us all back over to where she was seated and calmly said, "You do know what this is, don't you?" We listened intently. "This is spiritual warfare," she continued. "We have already lost six close family members over the last year and a half. The enemy is attacking us. We must be doing something right, because the enemy is taking notice. God is allowing these things to happen. So remember this: When warfare comes against the Evans family, we do not tuck our tails and run. No, we prepare to fight."

Her words echoed loudly in my heart like a drumbeat stirring me to rise. "If you are called to preach," she had continued, "you preach. If you are called to write, you write. If you are called to sing, you sing. If you are called to lead a Bible study, you lead it." As you can see, I really didn't have much of a choice that New Year's Eve night. I had to go preach. Lois would have it no other way.

So I showed up. Because the first thing to do when you need to man up is to show up.

I had planned to preach on James chapter 4 and how life is a vapor. That Scripture was so relevant to me that night, in light of everything that had transpired, that it flowed fresh from my heart. I had planned to challenge the members to submit to the will of God in their lives, day in and day out, but now more than just telling them, I realized I was showing them too. And looking back, with all the uncertainty and destruction so many have faced in the year 2020, I now know people needed that message lived out. They needed to see someone taking God seriously when all hope had gone. They needed a witness of what it looks like to honor God even when life hurts the worst it ever has.

Also, because so many of our church members had walked this journey with us through prayer, faith, cards, calls, visits, food, and even hour-long daily prayer vigils outside of our home for the last few months of Lois's life, I knew that showing up helped them to know their prayers had made a difference. I was still trusting God in the midst of deep pain. I hoped that sharing this reality with those I shepherd might also encourage them to keep going when life gets tough. I wanted them to see that basing their decisions on the will of

God as the dominant force in their thoughts is simply how we are to live as His followers.

Thus, in the dark room with curtains drawn on that cold and lonely New Year's Eve, my feet hit the floor, firmly. I rose. I stood. And I'm sure the devil said, "Oh crap, he's up."

We Are in This Together

Awakening our biblical manhood requires the commitment and the discipline to honor God in all we do. But what we often forget is that this determination is frequently formed in us over the course of our lives. It doesn't just magically appear.

I wasn't able to rise on my own strength alone that night during the most difficult time I have ever experienced. No, as I rose to go preach, all those who had poured their time and life into me over days, years, and decades were there helping me up. I felt their strength. I piggybacked on their faith. I heard them cheering me on. This is because nothing difficult we overcome ever rests solely on our own shoulders. That's one reason God emphasizes unity and the power of fellowship and discipleship throughout Scripture.

Growing up, I always had people in my life who invested in me in ways that allowed me to develop and mature into the man I am today. Early on, I had people who taught me a better way than what the urban atmosphere of Baltimore afforded me. They gave me a divine perspective as well as a broader viewpoint, which enabled me to go further than I thought I could on my own.

Most people who saw me growing up in a row house in urban Baltimore at the height of contemporary racial segregation may have written me off. But because some did not, and rather chose to invest in me through their own spiritual development and maturity, I was able to rise above the limitations society sought to impose.

God began this process by using my father's commitment to us as a family, especially when things got tough and money got tight. I also saw in him a profound dedication to the Word of God through his daily personal study, sharing it in prisons, handing out tracts on street corners, listening to the radio Bible teachers all day every day in our home, and later leading a church.

Then, God introduced a Jewish mentor and friend named Martin Resnick into my life to expand my thinking even more. From the age of sixteen on, I was given a bigger vision of the world through that relationship and Martin's influence on me as I worked for him. He birthed this bigger vision as he allowed me to gain experience in many areas. He spoke about concepts and dreams that encouraged me to think beyond my limited understanding at that time. I had never even considered attending college until Martin brought it up and offered to pay for it.

Another man who left his indelible stamp on my life was B. Sam Hart. This man of God, nationally renowned for evangelism, influenced me early on to step out of the circles of my immediate surroundings. When I was just eighteen years old, he gave me great confidence when he had confidence enough in me to send me alone to Guyana in South America. He sent me there to conduct the pre-fieldwork for one of his upcoming evangelistic crusades. His trust in me grew my belief in what I could do. Not only that, but the act of flying from the inner city of Baltimore, where African Americans were racially oppressed in the mid-1960s, to a nation where blacks held all positions of power, influence, and leadership opened my eyes to what could be. I saw a nation being run well by people who resembled me, and this gave me a fresh vision and hope.

As a result of these men investing in me early on, plus countless others I could name, such as Tom Skinner, Charles Ryrie, Zane Hodges, John Perkins, Charles Briscoe, Gene Getz, Ruben Conner, and Martin Hawkins, I became different from the culture at large. I began to be shaped by a kingdom world view that saw all of life falling under the overarching rule of God.

While my formative history is unique to me, my desire is that the principles in it would not be unique to many. Because what we need today are kingdom men who are willing to invest not only in their own personal growth and opportunities, but also in others. We need men who are willing to sacrifice the time and effort necessary to prioritize the unleashing of someone else's potential. We are in this thing called life together. That's how we make it. That's how we man up. That's how we change the world for God and for good.

As a refresher, or if you haven't read *Kingdom Man*, the definition of a kingdom man is *a male who visibly and consistently submits to the comprehensive relationship and rule of God, underneath the lordship of Jesus Christ, in every area of life.*[1] That must be the mind-set. A kingdom man accepts his responsibilities under God and faithfully carries them out. When he is faithful, God moves even pagan powers and other forces on earth to support him in doing his kingdom business. Jesus is the perfect example of a kingdom man in His earthly ministry (see John 17:4; 19:30; Philippians 3:7–14; Exodus 34:23–24; 1 Corinthians 11:3; and Genesis 18:19).

When a kingdom man lives according to his designed purpose, he joins with other men in influencing culture, politics, entertainment, and more through a process of intentional discipleship. This process produces kingdom disciples who then go and do the same. The process becomes cyclical, leading to multigenerational impact. A kingdom disciple can be defined as *a believer who takes part in the spiritual development of progressively learning to live all of life under the lordship of Jesus Christ and then seeks to replicate that process in others.* As this is done, God's kingdom agenda marches forward on earth.

Unless we rise up as kingdom men and assist other men to rise up as well, the culture will continue to devolve into the disaster it is quickly becoming. The catastrophe of manhood has reached every segment of our society. I don't need to list a plethora of statistics or stories to convince you of that. Anyone with their eyes open can easily recognize the precarious ledge upon which our society now stands.

If we intend to reverse the trends and stem the tide, it will take a group effort. As kingdom men, we must grab hold of those who need to be shown a better way, rather than write them off. As Paul told Timothy and many others under his influence, they were to follow his example, as he followed Christ (see 1 Corinthians 11:1 and Philippians 3:17).

Keep in mind that to have an example to follow means you must have someone setting one. This requires living in a spiritually mature manner and guiding others in how to do likewise. It takes both: ongoing personal discipline and intentional investment in others.

Why We Must Rise

Over and over God has called men to intervene on behalf of a dying land. Ezekiel 22:30 records it this way, "I searched for a man among them who would build up the wall and stand in the gap before Me for the land, so that I would not destroy it; but I found no one." The land had plenty of males, but God couldn't find a man. There's a big difference between being a male and being a kingdom man. You can be one without the other when you refuse to take responsibility under God.

While many of us are waiting on God to fix what is wrong, He is waiting on us to step up as men of faith and do what is right. He is waiting on men who don't just talk about faith but also walk in it. These are the men whose actions demonstrate that they truly believe in the God they claim to worship.

One way we do this is through intentional investments in relationships, exemplified in my life as I have just shared, as well as mutual learning in a spiritual context. In Exodus 34, we see this modeled for us when God called the men to come and meet with Him three times a year. In today's terminology, we could refer to this as a "Triannual Kingdom Conference." He did this because He wanted to instruct the men on how to live and think according to His standards. God promised the men that if they would take these meetings seriously, He would bring heaven's blessings of spiritual and physical prosperity into their lives, families, and nation (Exodus 23:17–31).

> While many of us are waiting on God to fix what is wrong, He is waiting on us to step up as men of faith and do what is right.

Following this collective time of mutual learning, they were sent back to their families and society in order to lead, defend, and influence it for God and for good.

God regularly instructed the men during times of convening on the crucial importance of both righteousness and justice. We will look at this more fully in chapter 8, "Get Along," but for our purposes right now, I want to introduce it. Righteousness is the moral standard that should govern every man's life and choices. Justice is the equitable application of God's moral standard as demonstrated in society. Many people identify with and commend the need for righteousness. But not as many understand why justice is similarly as vital. This has caused a condensed approach to discipleship and cultural influence by believers today, resulting in little overall societal impact.

Men, it is our role to seek out the manifestation of justice in the culture we live in. We are to rise up for those who cannot do so on their own (Micah 6:8; Proverbs 31:8). We do this by ensuring fair treatment and equal opportunities for the meeting of basic human needs such as education and employment. Without opportunity, many people lose hope. And one of the primary problems we are facing today is an increased sense of hopelessness. When a man loses hope, everything has been ripped from him. To take a man's hope is akin to taking his manhood. It cuts to the core of who we are as men because we have been designed to build, defend, create, cultivate, and govern (see Genesis 3).

That's why we need men who will be committed not only to evangelizing people for heaven but also to improving people's lives on earth. The kingdom of God involves both heaven and earth. We impact the spectrum of the culture at large when we influence individuals nearby.

In many ways, our failure to engage society strategically and spiritually has made us the cause of our own division, devolution, and destruction in our land, because we have not taken seriously this call to kingdom discipleship. But since we are the cause, we can also be the cure for the chaos we are experiencing today. If, and when, we rise up as kingdom men, we can usher in a new season of spiritual calm (see Leviticus 26:6; Judges 3:11).

Chosen for Greatness

You have been created by God with a specific post He wants you to fulfill and a purpose He wants you to live out. He has scouted you, pursued you, and drafted you for His kingdom team. You have a divinely orchestrated reason for your manhood. Now, I know the culture wants to give you a whole slew of other reasons for being a man, but God says clearly that He created you for something great. You have been drafted for the purposes of God. We gain insight into these purposes when we look at God's choosing of Abraham in Genesis 18:19 (NIV):

> For I have chosen him, so that he will direct his children and his household after him to keep the way of the LORD by doing what is right and just, so that the LORD will bring about for Abraham what he has promised him.

Just as God chose Abraham, He has chosen you. If you are saved and part of the body of Christ, God has a divine design for your life. This purpose will bring about the furtherance of His glory and the expansion of His kingdom.

Granted, that purpose may seem elusive right now. You may have to search for it as the Avengers searched for the Infinity Stones. But if you will search for it, you will find it. I'll give you a hint as to how. As you draw closer to God, He makes known His purposes for you. He enlightens you as to why you are here on earth and what role you are to play. Proverbs 20:5 (NIV) puts it like this: "The purposes of a person's heart are deep waters, but one who has insight draws them out."

God has placed your purpose in you, in seed form. You grow that seed through an intentional pursuit of Him. Your purpose will be revealed to you only as you get to know God more fully. When you learn His ways like an athlete learns the plays, desires, and instincts of a coach, you will align yourself with all that is needed in order to maximize your potential.

Once you come to realize that God has already chosen you for success—He has given you your own number—you can take confidence in the assurance of His carrying it out. He has situated you to live victoriously as a kingdom man. Your effort involves aligning yourself within His grid and with His design.

God will bring about your greatness. You don't need to force it, manipulate to get it, or obsessively work toward it. God will do it himself. We see this principle play out in the latter part of the verse we just looked at, Genesis 18:19 (NIV): "So that the LORD will bring about for Abraham what he has promised him."

God will bring about for you what He has promised you as well. Your part involves alignment and obedience. God takes care of the rest. Even the greatness.

We see this in looking closely at what God promised Abraham in verses 17–18: "The LORD said, 'Shall I hide from Abraham what I am about to do, since Abraham will surely become a great and mighty nation, and in him all the nations of the earth will be blessed?'"

God's promise for Abraham in two words? *Greatness* and *influence.* Through Abraham's greatness, all the nations of the earth would be blessed. He became a multigenerational man of impact. God desires nothing less for you as well. In Christ, we are all recipients of Abraham's purpose lived out in his promise. We read,

> The promises were spoken to Abraham and to his seed. Scripture does not say "and to seeds," meaning many people, but "and to your seed," meaning one person, who is Christ.
>
> Galatians 3:16 NIV

> If you belong to Christ, then you are Abraham's seed, and heirs according to the promise.
>
> Galatians 3:29 NIV

Abraham's promise of greatness and influence is ours as well. It's yours. Own it. To be great under God naturally includes influencing all those around you. When you think of Tom Brady or Peyton Manning, you don't just think of somebody who played football. You think of someone who influenced the entire game of football, and their team. Why? Because they left their mark. Their mere presence elevated the players around them, and as a result, all were able to achieve more individually and collectively than many thought they ever would.

We are to do the same.

I realize that many of you who have picked up this book may be at a place where you have made mistakes, you live with regret, or you have simply failed to maximize the giftings and skills God has given you. It could be that life hasn't been fair. You read *Kingdom Man*. You understand a call to greatness. But you just don't know how you could possibly get there yourself, not with all that is missing or messed up in your life.

If that's you, I want to remind you that greatness has more to do with heart than skill, just as success in football has more to do with effort than talent. Those who put in the work rise to the top. Those who arrive early and stay late create the historic stories with their games. Those who don't allow personal disadvantages to play out as disadvantages are the ones we later refer to as legends.

Tom Brady didn't get drafted until the sixth round, but he has won six Super Bowl championships (at the time of this writing.) Brady didn't allow what people thought of him to determine the effort he would put into the game he calls his passion.

This principle ought to ring true for kingdom men too. It is your willingness to show up in life day in and day out, be present in relationships, put forth the effort on the job, commit, give, apply diligence, study the Word, invest in others, and the like that will shape your own legacy of distinction.

Show up.

Be present.

Stay consistent.

If you do those three things, you will leave a legacy of excellence. After all, legacy is the culmination of a million middle moments done well. It's not about that Hail Mary or kickoff return for a touchdown. It's the small things. The consistent conversations. The wise choices that add up over time. That's what creates the heritage you leave behind.

Greatness Is Coming

You may not recognize the name Shaquem Griffin, but I imagine you'd recognize him if you saw him playing a game in the NFL. That's because Griffin was the first player to ever achieve something momentous in the

NFL, or any professional sport, by playing it without one of his hands. Shaquem lost his hand to amputation when he was only four years old.

He was born with amniotic band syndrome, and his family opted to remove his hand entirely after finding him in the kitchen one night trying to cut off his deformed, painful fingers with a knife. Not hesitating at all, his mom took him to the hospital the very next day for the surgery.[2]

While he was still in the womb, his parents had been given the option of having the doctors try to move the fibrous tissue wrapped around his hand. But they knew this could also lead to it wrapping around Shaquem's neck or possibly his twin brother Shaquill's. That was a risk they were not willing to take.[3] So they decided to keep it where it was and trust God.

Both parents made another decision at that time as well. As they later stated, they decided that they would not parent Shaquem any differently than their other children. They would "never let him consider his condition a hindrance."[4] That wise choice only strengthened him.

Yet, if we are honest, few of us might have been able to make that same choice Shaquem's parents did on how to raise him. Most of us may have sought to compensate somehow for his missing hand. And we wouldn't have blamed him for adopting a victim mind-set in life. In fact, many parents in that same situation might have gone on to adopt a victim mind-set for themselves as well.

Who would argue that navigating the daily demands of life without a hand might be considered justifiable grounds for blaming God, at least a little? Yet neither Shaquem nor his parents chose to live by that mentality. As a result, he not only became a great enough athlete to land a starting role in college, but he also created history when he went on to be drafted in the NFL.

The draft call came from the Seahawks while Shaquem was in the bathroom, fittingly enough. I say that it's fitting because the context of a bathroom is where many of us were first introduced to Shaquem and his inspirational story.

You may recognize him from the highly popular and inspirational commercial he did for Gillette after he was drafted. This commercial has evoked many tears in viewers over the years. It began with a scene portraying a much younger Shaquem and his dad in the bathroom as his dad taught him how to shave with only one hand. The commercial then went on to show other scenes of his father teaching him how to do whatever else he needed to do in order to overcome and to achieve his dreams, including playing football. The title of the commercial is fitting as well: "Shaquem Griffin: Your Best Never Comes Easy."[5]

What Shaquem's father, and those around him, taught him obviously worked because Coach Carroll later had this to say on the Seahawks' decision to draft a player without a hand:

> "We looked at that very closely, to try to determine is there a factor that makes it obvious that maybe we shouldn't take him. We thought he overcame all of the odds and was able to make the plays."[6]

Shaquem had, against all odds, mastered a sport that sees less than 1 percent of high school senior players make it to the NFL.[7] A sport of dexterity, mobility, and the obvious use of players' hands. But Shaquem knew his dream he had worked so hard to achieve was in God's hands. He had this to say to an ESPN reporter when asked about the wait immediately after he got the call:

> "It was tough—I'm not going to lie to you. . . . Seeing all them guys picked in front of me, and just falling back and knowing that . . . I did everything that I was supposed to do. But, you know, it was in God's hands."[8]

The reporter and crew from ESPN had gathered at Shaquem's house the day of the draft in order to capture this momentous occasion, which he chose to share with his twin, Shaquill, already a cornerback for the Seahawks.

"What does it say that you're gonna now have an opportunity to play with your brother Shaquill?" the reporter asked.

"It's going to bring back everything we ever wanted," Shaquem replied, tears in his eyes and, by his own admission, barely even able to speak or breathe. He continued, "This is everything we prayed for. This is everything we worked for. This is everything we stayed true to who we are [for]. And now that I got the opportunity to be back with him, it's only going to mean greatness."

The reporter then turned to his twin brother to hear from him. "Just to see us make it this far and to see where he's going and where he's about to go. It's a humbling experience, and I'm definitely enjoying the ride," Shaquill said as he stood there crying.

"Why is this emotional for you?" the reporter asked. He replied,

"A lot of people really don't understand what we really went through, and you know, you hear the stories, you get a little brief summary, of what we talked about or what he kind of went through, but it's so much more, and to see your dream come true . . . the way it did today? To get a chance to play with each other again, it means the world to me and I know it means the world to him. That's why I'm so emotional. I don't think I cried at my draft day, and I couldn't hold it, I just couldn't hold it. I'm excited."

The reporter then asked the question meant for us all: "To all the people who are doubted in life, who are told that their dreams can't come true, what would you say to them?"

Shaquem answered boldly, "Just keep working . . . if you keep working, your dream will come true. And this is not the end of my road; it's only just the beginning, and I'm going to keep proving people wrong."

I'm sure most of you will agree with me in saying that Shaquem has nothing left to prove. He has already proven plenty simply through this major overcoming accomplishment. Regardless, he keeps on fighting the odds. Staring down the opposition. Rising as a champion each day and every play. "Greatness is coming," Shaquem managed to say as the interview came to a close.[9]

Yes, greatness is coming.

It's a strong statement indicating future success. But I don't think I'm going out on a limb to say that for many of us who have striven to leap the hurdles of hurt, loss, regret, and disadvantages in life, the statement might also be this:

Greatness has already arrived.

It's here. It's in him. It's in each of us. Right now. In fact, Shaquem Griffin wasn't just chosen for the greatness to come, he was chosen because of the greatness already exhibited within him.

Greatness is in every one of you who has picked up this book, seeking to make your next decision better than your last. It's in each of you who strives to learn how to live life in wisdom while leaving a legacy of faith. It's in each of you who awakens to rise up in your God-given capacity to influence a world in desperate need of hope. Greatness is yours right now.

Every day, in every way, as you barrel through the enemy's line and tear through the opposition, greatness is yours to live out. Once you realize greatness is not something out there and out of reach, but it is to be demonstrated in the daily tasks of your life—it is to be your routine—you will reach the end zone of eternal gain.

> Once you realize greatness is not something out there and out of reach, but it is to be demonstrated in the daily tasks of your life—it is to be your routine—you will reach the end zone of eternal gain.

Calling Our Culture to Rise Up

While my book *Kingdom Man* was written to challenge men to define manhood as God intended it to be, I'm writing this book both to equip men individually to overcome what is holding them back from living it out and to empower men collectively for multigenerational impact.

We will begin by identifying and addressing common issues that keep us down or limit the full expression of our potential. I'll spend time looking at this in the remainder of part one as well as part two. Then we will explore how to rise up collectively through principles of life impact and mutual investment and accountability, which we will look at together in part three.

I've chosen to focus so heavily on discipleship and authentic values transfer in this book because one of the ways Satan has successfully restrained forward momentum of kingdom warriors is by keeping us siloed.

We have embraced a compartmentalized view of Christianity, with each of us often focusing more on our own lives, plans, platforms, and personal desires. This leaves little room for any thought on the overarching kingdom agenda. I define the kingdom agenda as *the visible manifestation of the comprehensive rule of God over every area of life.*[10]

No war was ever won when soldiers fought separately based on their own goals and strategies. Until and unless we recognize and address this, we will stay stuck playing defense—never advancing the ball into the end zone of eternal impact.

I'm sure you are aware of the great strides many entities have made in our nation and around the world because they have united on a common message and goal. A 2017 Gallup poll reported that only 4.5 percent of all Americans identified openly as LGBT.[11] And yet that 4.5 percent has been hugely successful in pushing through policies, laws, and even overall cultural trends and messaging in arts, entertainment, and education. This intentional and highly partnered pursuit of promoting their unbiblical agenda has advanced their cause exponentially in a short time.

Compare this to a 2019 Pew Research study, which found that roughly 65 percent of Americans call themselves Christians.[12] And yet with such a high number, Christianity continues to face losses in our land as time moves on. Losses in influence, rights, and even perception.

I find it alarming that in America we have more Christian books than you could ever read, more Christian television than you could ever watch, more Christian radio than you could ever listen to, more Christian social media sites than you could ever visit, church services on Sunday and on Wednesday—and yet we are a nation of dry bones (see Ezekiel 37). We are a nation in a valley. We are a nation of mess—asleep, ineffective, and watching from the sidelines. The spiritual situation in our culture of men has led to vast social disintegration. We have dry men contributing to dry marriages composing dry families attending dry churches while living in a dry land.

And this is so because an authentic spiritual life doesn't come through rituals, budgets, programs, buildings, or even religion. Spiritual life, power, and strength come from the Spirit. The closer we are to the Spirit, the more abundant life we experience and the more influence we carry out (John 10:10; 15:7). The further we are from Christ's Spirit, the more death and decay we experience.

Men, it's past time that we learn how to identify and heal from whatever it is that keeps us dry individually and segmented collectively. Both have made us ineffective for the kingdom of God. We must intentionally pursue personal growth and cross-relational discipleship if we are to have much left of our Christian heritage to leave as a legacy.

It is absolutely critical that we own the issues plaguing us on many fronts today. As kingdom men, we must own our roles in pointing each other to the one true King. We must own the responsibility of calling a culture in decline back to Christ. It's time we awaken not only ourselves but the culture at large, so we will take to the field and overcome the opposition at hand.

My challenge to you as we set out to go through this book and these life principles together is this: No matter how deep the pain or difficult the challenges, do not give in to apathy, disillusionment, or despair. Open the curtains of your soul. Let the light in. Sit up. Let your feet hit the floor, firmly. And then, stand. Let's make the devil mumble underneath his breath as he witnesses an army of kingdom men rising, "Oh crap, they're up."

TWO

DRY BONES CAN DANCE

Monday night. Paul Brown Stadium. The air rumbled with its own undercurrents of war, threatening to unleash a torrent of terror like tornadic winds beneath a steamy midwestern sky. Never mind the sixty-five thousand onlookers thirsty for the first taste of blood in this modern-day gladiator fight. The atmosphere itself taunted more loudly, indicating it might explode under the weight of this half-century history of battles without end.

It was the Steelers. And the Bengals. Say no more. To infer that these two teams have perhaps the fiercest rivalry in all of the NFL would garner little pushback from anyone. They play mean. Both lines loom in front of each other like ferocious bullies. At times, you can even smell the hint of hatred spilling over from their hearts. The grit and grime of a regular football game holds nothing on this squaring off of sheer savagery. Vicious, violent, legal, and illegal hits make these sixty minutes of combat barely more than an exercise in brutality.

There have been broken jaws. Bone-crushing tackles. Even a separated shoulder—in a playoff game, nonetheless. A knee driven downward into an already downed quarterback will do just that.[1]

That's why a seemingly innocuous tackle in the opening minutes of the game barely drew a glance from the crowd. At first, that is.

The camera began to pan away, then quickly returned. But I'm getting ahead of myself.

If you were watching the game, you probably remember this play clearly, or at least you remember your reaction to it. If you weren't, I'll set the stage:

Monday Night Football, December 4, 2017. The Bengals stared down a 2nd and 5 with roughly eleven minutes left in the first quarter. Scoreless game. Quarterback Andy Dalton dropped back for a quick pass to rookie Josh Malone. Nothing unusual here. Malone grabbed the ball and braced himself for what most expected to be a pretty normal hit. Short gain for the Bengals. But a huge loss for the Steelers. Here's why: The moment the crown of defensive lineman Ryan Shazier's helmet hit the fairly open receiver, everything changed. Shazier fell to the ground, immediately grabbing his back. Somehow, he managed to roll himself over, his right hand then grasping the air as if it were thick enough to hold on to. His legs never moved. The entire time.

Moments turned into minutes. Minutes dragged on like millennia. One by one, players dropped to a knee. Coach Tomlin paced the sideline looking more like a friend who had just seen his sandlot buddy get pummeled. Yet as prayers continued to rise up, Shazier remained down. Eventually, the medical personnel strapped him to a stretcher and carried him to the nearby emergency cart. No thumbs-up came from the former Ohio standout as they carted him off the field. Instead, he buried his head in both hands, overcome by the magnitude of the mess he was in.

Reportedly, prior to the game, quarterback Ben Roethlisberger had told an ESPN commentator that this rivalry with the Bengals concerned him. "I worry about players getting injured on both sides when this game is played," he said, specifically referring to the Steelers-Bengals style of play, "because sometimes it crosses the line."[2] The game would go on to see a number of other injuries as well. Taunting. Illegal hits. Sheer animosity filled each play. It got so bad that former NFL quarterback Troy Aikman tweeted toward the end of the game, "This game is hard to watch for a number of reasons. Terrible for the NFL and the game of football overall."[3]

But despite the terror of an overly violent night, more tender emotions rose up as well. Many of the Steelers' tough, hardened players had a difficult time holding back tears for their teammate Shazier. Grown men cried on the sidelines. In fact, safety Mike Mitchell said of Vince Williams,

"I don't think [he] stopped crying until after halftime, and that's one of the most gangster dudes on the team. People had to grab him by the face mask and be like, 'Yo, you're the middle linebacker now. You can't be sniffling.'"[4] I can see a few of the opposition players looking at him before each play like the coach in the movie *A League of Their Own*: "Come on, man! There's no crying in football!" But crying took place that night.

The Steelers would go on to win the game, which isn't surprising based on the past. Overall, they lead the rivalry 65–35 at the time of this writing. In addition, the Steelers have been ranked as the second winningest team for the bulk of this century, while the Bengals tend to hover around twentieth.[5] The Steelers-Bengals game is rarely a competition to see who is best. Stats and data have already logged that reality in the long run. But even so, it remains a hard-fought war waged with abandonment, for whatever reasons motivate both teams.

Shazier would remain overnight in Cincinnati in a hospital for some tests before being transferred back to Pittsburgh for a spinal stabilization surgery. This surgery would leave him paralyzed for weeks. The physicians assigned to his care warned him that he would never fully recover.[6] They told him he most likely would never even walk again.

But Shazier had never been one to listen to naysayers or a negative crowd. Born with a rare autoimmune disorder called alopecia, Shazier learned early on how to tune out negativity. He's walked the road less traveled all his life. Alopecia is a disease wherein the body attacks its own hair follicles. Bald pretty much from birth, Shazier discovered at a young age not to let what other people had to say affect him too much. His parents taught him how to respond to those who criticized him, put him down, or pointed him out. They taught him to shut it down through laughter.[7]

As a result, Shazier had developed a healthy sense of humor over his twenty-six years of life. Nothing evidenced this so clearly as Coach Tomlin's comments to the news media just hours after seeing him that December night. Shazier was in "really good spirits," Tomlin stated without hesitation, adding that Shazier is a "tough guy."[8] "Really good spirits" isn't what you'd expect to hear about a man who was just told he would probably be crippled for life. But Shazier maintained a positive outlook, which would prove to serve him well.

Over the course of the next year, Shazier spent countless sweat-filled hours in rehab defying the doctor's prognosis that he would never stand on his own again. He posted regularly on social media thanking his fans and friends for support. Shazier wanted everyone to remain optimistic like he was and believe in his healing. He knew the power of prayer. He knew the power of the mind.

After only six months, Shazier demonstrated the results of his dedication coupled with everyone's prayers. He walked across the stage of the NFL Draft, hand in hand with his fiancée, Michelle, who had proven to be a constant cheerleader and encouragement to him on his long road to recovery. They shared the stage together as he announced the Steelers' first draft pick of the year. It was an emotional moment for many, especially for Shazier and the love of his life.

And then, after only three hundred and some odd days following his spinal injury, Shazier did something that left all his fans and supporters amazed. He walked unassisted onto the very field where he had lost most of his physical freedoms in that horrific play.[9] Each step on that turf in Cincinnati created a rumbling of cheers from the crowd like a thunderous ovation by God himself. Even the Bengals fans applauded.

Doctors had once told this man that he probably would never walk again. But Shazier walked with his head held high that night. In fact, a few months later he would do more than walk. Shazier would dance again.

Just a year and a half after his career-ending spinal injury, Shazier married his best friend and faithful rehab cheerleader, Michelle, in an all-out celebration attended by celebrities and Steelers alike. Following the vows, Shazier cut more than the cake. He cut a rug. Dancing with his new bride, he had the last laugh after all. Headlines peppered the papers the next morning with what felt like a collective end zone celebration in what had once loomed as a national loss.

Ryan Shazier Gets Married, Is Able to Dance (CBS Sports)
Ryan Shazier Dances at His Wedding (ProFootballTalk)
Ryan Shazier Dances at His Wedding . . . After Severe Spinal Cord Injury (*People* magazine)
Steelers LB Dances with His New Bride (ESPN)

The whole country, and even the world, marveled at this man's moves. After all, dancing takes place in the end zone when a football team scores. Shazier had indeed scored on behalf of himself and his wife through his recovery. He scored for all of us. In the way he retained his dignity and delight in spite of tragedy, he reminded all of us who have ever faced an insurmountable opponent of our own that though life may knock us down, we can rise again. It doesn't get much more redemptive than rising from the remains of personal loss to dance to the beat of a better drum.

If you follow Shazier on social media, you'll still catch him putting up videos of himself dancing with his wife and his kids. You'll also hear him routinely praising God for the miracle of his restoration and the great value of life. Interestingly enough, Shazier remained a Steeler for some time too. The respectable ownership of one of the most loyal football teams in the league kept him on staff as a retired or inactive player for a number of years. They committed to stand by Shazier as he found his new path in life. Many fans saw him on the sidelines or in the stadium of most Steelers games, a living symbol of strength for his fellow warriors to witness and emulate.

Shazier's story may not resemble each of our own. Most of us are not high-round defensive draft picks for one of the nation's most respected defensive football teams. Most of us don't have sixty-five thousand fans cheering for us as we walk out onto a field, or head into work, or face our personal oppositions. Neither do we have that many prayers going up for us when we get knocked down or suffer personal setbacks. But his story still serves as a reminder of what is possible when a man chooses to believe the best in a hopeless situation.

Hopeless scenarios surround many men today. We find them in Scripture too. You won't find one much more hopeless, though, than the biblical story I want us to look at in this chapter. It's a story about awakening manhood, literally. It's an account concerning the rising up of formerly strong and mighty warriors who had lost it all.

The Valley of Dry Bones[10]

The story is set in the period known as the Babylonian exile. In the first group of Judean captives taken by the Babylonians (2 Kings 24:10–16) around 597 BC, we come across a young man named Ezekiel. Ezekiel and his fellow deportees had been forced to their knees, crippled by an oppressive enemy regime. They didn't see a way out. They may have examined their own nation's history and recalled what had happened to their sister kingdom, Israel, which, when deported over a century earlier, ultimately fell into demise. In fact, she lost her identity to the point that she became known as the lost tribes of Israel.

Ezekiel and his countrymen in exile suffered loss on many levels—the loss of their city, temple, identity, traditions, rituals, and once-lauded Davidic rule. As a result, a number of people even lost their faith. A major collapse had occurred, and no one offered any real solutions for how to fix it.

Dreams had been cut short. They were lulled into the trance of despair. They buried their faces in their hands as hopelessness filled their hearts, where passion and pursuit had once beat strong.

That's why God sent a wake-up call who went by the name of Ezekiel. It was time for the men to get up. To rise. To stand again. And God was about to show them how through this young man some may have called Zeke for short.

First, God ushered him to an ossuary the Israelites had set aside as a place for bones to be gathered before they were buried. Ezekiel stood before this valley of dry, dismembered bones. It doesn't get any more hopeless than that. In fact, for an extended amount of time, these bones had been left to bake in the unrelenting sun. According to Ezekiel there were "a great many bones on the floor of the valley" and they were "very dry" (Ezekiel 37:2 NIV). Since these bones represented the nation's army (see v. 10), they likewise represented a nation of defeated men. In fact, at this point the entire nation was represented by the failure of this army.

As you know, a valley is a low place. It's that place where you have to look up just to see bottom. These bones lay in this valley jumbled together like too many cords tucked away in a drawer. Nothing was connected as it should have been. Nothing was attached where it belonged. Bones remained piled on each other in chaos. Sound familiar? To a degree, it should to most of us.

Not that I expect anyone to identify with dismembered bones, but many men today live dismembered lives. They don't see hope. They are drowning in a sea of despair surrounded by emptiness. The skies are always cloudy, yet the scorching sun still somehow damages their souls. No light shines at the end of the tunnel unless it's the light of an oncoming train.

Maybe that's you. Maybe that's why you've picked up this book. Maybe you feel like you need your own wake-up call in life. You're just plain tired, dry, barren, and shut down. The fire and the passion are gone. Life seems to ebb away day after day. Your drive, which at one time was strong, now relies on mere fumes. Your get-up-and-go has gotten up and gone.

If truth be told, many of the men reading this book don't even know how much further or longer they can go. I know this from the sheer volume of phone calls, counseling requests, letters, emails, social media comments, and direct messages that come my way. When questions come up on how to cure the plague of missing manhood in our nation that leads to so many societal ills, most responses come with a shrug of the shoulders and Ezekiel's own words, which I paraphrase, "Only God knows" (Ezekiel 37:3). That's a polite way of saying, "I give up. I don't think any of us knows how to solve this. At all." We read the context of Ezekiel's statement in the opening verses of Ezekiel 37:

> The hand of the LORD was upon me, and He brought me out by the Spirit of the LORD and set me down in the middle of the valley; and it was full of bones. He caused me to pass among them round about, and behold, there were very many on the surface of the valley; and lo, they were very dry. He said to me, "Son of man, can these bones live?" And I answered, "O Lord GOD, You know."
>
> vv. 1–3

Ezekiel didn't have an answer for God other than that God himself knew if this dead nation of men could rise again. Similarly, many of us are lacking the answers or assurance of belief that what seems dead in our lives, homes, and nation today could ever recover. Perhaps it's a dead marriage. Could be a dead career. Might be a dead mentality. We are certainly witnessing a dead moral framework and deadened society. And whatever it is that has caused so many to lie limp on the ground seems to have sucked away hope for a solution as well.

I would argue that is because it's hard to fix a problem when you don't know, or choose to ignore, the cause. Whenever you are looking for a cure, you must address the cause. Far too many laymen, pastors, and politicians are doing patchwork on symptoms rather than dealing with the systemic roots that have caused the decay. If we are ever to get our lives, homes, churches, and nation right, we have to address the spiritual causes beneath the brokenness we are experiencing.

> If we are ever to get our lives, homes, churches, and nation right, we have to address the spiritual causes beneath the brokenness we are experiencing.

The good news is we can gain insight into our own culture by looking at what caused this valley to be filled with dry bones. We're told the cause in Ezekiel 36:16–21.

Then the word of the LORD came to me saying, "Son of man, when the house of Israel was living in their own land, they defiled it by their ways and their deeds; their way before Me was like the uncleanness of a woman in her impurity. Therefore I poured out My wrath on them for the blood which they had shed on the land, because they had defiled it with their idols. Also I scattered them among the nations and they were dispersed throughout the lands. According to their ways and their deeds I judged them. When they came to the nations where they went, they profaned My holy name, because it was said of them, 'These are the people of the LORD; yet they have come out of His land.' But I had concern for My holy name, which the house of Israel had profaned among the nations where they went."

Let me say it plainly: The reason they were dried up in a valley for an extended time was because their disobedience had created distance. That distance from God led to their dryness. They had started off in their own land, yet they chose to rebel. God then exiled them to the other nations. As a result, they became spiritually estranged. They had been removed from fellowship with God, and during this time of removal, they had devolved into a nation with a valley of dry bones.

Similarly, men, if you are dry—spiritually, emotionally, relationally, or in any other way—it is most likely because you are distant from God. And distance is always a result of disobedience. Now, I know that we all have dry moments or dry times. A man can face a slump here or setback there. I'm not talking about that. But if you find yourself living in a dry valley where every single day you wake up to no motivation, no passion, and no spiritual fervor, it is because you have become distant from God. One thing leads to prolonged distance from God: failing to align under the rule of the King.

As verse 18 says in the passage we just looked at, Israel's men had become disobedient through their idol worship. Idolatry is intimacy with an image. It's not necessarily bowing down to a carved statue stuck on a pole. No, an idol is anything that usurps God's rightful rule in your life. Idols come in all shapes and sizes. What's more, they can even be found in the church. After all, the Israelites had defiled their land with idols. As verse 18 states, they were still in their land when they turned toward the idols.

Idolatry is not just an out-there concept in a distant land. Many people worship idols while attending church. I say that because idolatry centers on alignment: That which you align your thoughts, words, and actions under is what you value most.

Have you ever wondered how we can have all these churches and all these books and all these songs, programs, seminars, huddle groups, Bible studies, radio broadcasts, podcasts, and more and yet still have all this mess? There are idols everywhere; that's how. Somebody, or something, has been brought into God's realm of rule, and there is no room for two kings in any sovereign land.

The Israelites had turned to other sources to meet their needs, to entertain them, to solve their problems and offer solutions. As a result, the nation symbolically lay dead in a wasteland of dismembered destinies.

How Badly Do You Want to Get Up?

These dry bones now lay there representing the hope of Israel, or lack thereof. By this point in their exile, the people had given up. They had thrown in the towel. They could no longer see a way out of the darkness that engulfed them. Their sin had worked itself out in their society, which led to their being taken captive and living as exiles in Babylon (Ezekiel 36:19–20). The Israelites found themselves in a situation with no solution. Their spiritual disconnection had led to a social catastrophe. What's worse is they were so far removed from God that they could no longer readily identify the cause of the effect.

Men, when we fail to make the connection between the spiritual and the social, we fail to seek the solution that can bring real and lasting impact. We fail to address the spiritual root of the physical mayhem at hand. As a result, we remain in a valley of spiritual, emotional, relational, or even vocational dryness, unable to rise at all.

That's the problem related to so much of what we're facing as men in our nation today as well. Yet in the midst of Israel's problem, we find a promise—a promise we also can look toward. I'm getting a little ahead of myself, but I think it's important to give the endgame in order to better illuminate the process to that promise. God states His goal clearly in Ezekiel 37:12–13 when He says to Ezekiel,

> "Therefore prophesy and say to them, 'Thus says the Lord God, "Behold, I will open your graves and cause you to come up out of your graves, My people; and I will bring you into the land of Israel. Then you will know that I am the Lord, when I have opened your graves and caused you to come up out of your graves, My people."'"

God gave a promise that He alone would open the graves and cause life to exist where death had once dominated. Now, last I checked, if you are dead and you come up out of a grave, that's a supernatural arising. That's awakening from a pretty solid and long sleep. Thus, the good news we find from this final promise God made is that no matter how dry you are or how dry your situation may be, those bones can live again.

If you are dry spiritually, you can live again.

If your marriage has been dried up for years, or even decades, it can thrive again.

If your circumstances are dry or your career is a wasteland, it can rise and prosper again.

Men, if God can take an ossuary of dry bones and cause it to pulsate with life, how much more can He do for you in your dry situation? The question is never *Can God do it?* The question is always *How badly do you want it?*

The Process to the Promise

Let's head back a few verses to identify the process God used to get these men to their promise. In Ezekiel 37:4–5, we unearth God's two-part plan to get those bones to rise up again. This plan included both His word and His Spirit.

First, we read, "Prophesy over these bones and say to them, 'O dry bones, hear the word of the LORD'" (v. 4).

Secondly, it says, "Thus says the Lord GOD to these bones, 'Behold, I will cause breath to enter you that you may come to life'" (v. 5).

For starters, God told Ezekiel to speak His Word into their dead situation. He said, "Hear the word of the LORD." God didn't want Ezekiel to tell them what Ezekiel thought or to give human ideas and opinions. He didn't ask Ezekiel to give them the popular viewpoint of the day, cater to their emotional well-being, provide a psychological analysis, or take a Gallup poll. He didn't even ask Ezekiel to tell them something designed to make them feel good. Ezekiel wasn't called to write something to land him on the *New York Times* bestsellers list, snag a seat on a popular show, or end up on the cover of a magazine. Rather, God asked Ezekiel to give the dry bones His truth in His Word. It's truth that sets a man free. And now that they had reached this abysmal point of collective paralysis, God knew that they would be willing to listen to truth once again.

Thus, God started their awakening with His Word. As a result, the bones came together. But as you know, connected bones moving all around without life in them are monsters. It's a bad scene from a B-rated zombie film. God's promise involved two parts, because not only did the bones need to come back together, but the bones also needed life to be restored.

So after the truth of His Word, God gave them the power of His Spirit. The original Hebrew word translated as "breath" in verse five is the word God used to identify His Spirit at the beginning of the creation process in Genesis 1:2. With His Spirit, God *breathed* new life into the dead bones. In biology, we would call that a revival. In theology, we call it the same.

Through this combination of the Word and the Spirit, God brought about the start of an awakening in the land. He ushered in a revival, both literal and spiritual. In verses 7–8 and 10 of Ezekiel 37, we read about this awakening. We see how God's Word and His Spirit birthed a movement of an army of kingdom men rising (emphasis added):

> So I prophesied as I was commanded; and as I prophesied, there was a noise, and behold, a rattling; and the bones came together, bone to its bone. And I looked, and behold, sinews were on them, and flesh grew and skin covered them. . . . And the breath came into them, and they came to life and stood on their feet, an *exceedingly great army*.

How long had those bones been dry in that pit? Years. The nation had been out of God's will for a very long time. But God can turn things around on a dime when it's time. When you have reached the end of yourself, you are poised for a sudden and supernatural rising.

You've probably had your car battery go out at some point. I know I have. Standing there looking at that battery won't do a bit of good. Talking to the battery won't change a thing either. It's only when you take a set of cables to connect your dead battery to someone else's live battery that you get the spark you need to drive. That battery gets recharged through the transference of life from another.

Similarly, the only way that we as kingdom men will experience personal awakening and rise up to fulfill our destinies is through connecting to God's living Word and Spirit. Both are essential before we can experience the spiritual resurrection God offers. It's through His life transferred to us that we will have a transformative influence on our homes, communities, nation, and even world.

After all, a valley of dry bones is the last place anyone would think to look for an exceedingly great army. It's hard to be a soldier and fight to save someone else when you can't even save yourself. Yet from the Israelites' scattered and dead mess of dry bones, God raised up an army to advance His kingdom agenda and bring life to others in the land.

Stuff that had lain there rotting and dead, confused, disassociated—like puzzle pieces in a box—began to connect and soon became the living portrait of a vast army. The Word of God put the pieces together in order, connecting bone with bone, muscle with muscle, and sinew with sinew. Likewise, God's Word orders our own lives when we read and apply it.

> The only way that we as kingdom men will experience personal awakening and rise up to fulfill our destinies is through connecting to God's living Word and Spirit.

When men lead families who then live in alignment with His truth, and when men serve in churches that then function in alignment with His precepts, the nation feels the effect. It is when kingdom men—as individuals, business owners, employees, politicians, fathers, medical workers, preachers, and the like—all align with God and His Word that we experience order in the land.

As we move forward in this journey together through this book, I want you to focus on the promise. Take a lesson from Ryan Shazier and keep your spirits high. If your bones are in the valley and there seems to be no human solution, God has a promise for you. Those bones can rise again.

You don't have to give up, give in, or throw in the towel. You don't have to run away from your responsibilities. I know you may feel like it. I understand that the bones you are dealing with may have been dry for an extended period and you may have lost all hope of ever regaining your fire, passion, and drive. But before you hang up the cleats, remember what God told the prophet: "I will . . . cause you to come up out of your graves" (Ezekiel 37:12).

But remember, only the Spirit of God himself can pull you up out of that casket. That means the top priority in your life right now ought to be cultivating and growing in your relationship with God's Word and getting to know Him better. As you do, you'll awaken. You'll stand. You'll walk, unassisted.

Nothing, and no one, is too far gone from God's powerful hand. He wants you to know that. In fact, that's why God does the supernatural. He revives and restores so that you will know Him more. God doesn't mince His words or hide His motivations. He tells us clearly in verse 13, "*Then you will know* that I am the LORD, when I have opened your graves and caused you to come up out of your graves, My people" (emphasis added).

When whatever you are facing gets turned around, there will be no question who did it. You will know God for yourself. After all, it's one thing to hear about a resurrection of a hopeless situation; it's another thing entirely to experience it.

THREE

A TALE OF TWO MEN

The winding river stretches some 855 miles through fertile lands and sweeping slopes, having originated from the Great Himalayas. Life flows from this river, providing drinking water for more than 50 million people as well as irrigation.[1] Although severely polluted at this point, the Yamuna River remains one of the most cherished and celebrated sources of water in all of India.

That is, until monsoon season hits. From June to September, rain can come on suddenly in this region, causing rivers to rise and shores to expand. Delight can just as suddenly become despair when gratitude for refreshing showers gets set aside as people scatter to find shelter from flooded streets. It is not uncommon for water to rise to waist height in the streets. In 2017, millions of people were displaced and 1,200 died due to a tragic series of floods.[2]

Monsoons are nothing to mess with. Preparations and awareness can prevent loss of life. Unfortunately, though, preparations often are in short supply. That's why in 2010, a multifloor building in the Lalita Park area of New Delhi collapsed catastrophically under the stress of the shifting sand. The hundreds of people living there scrambled for safety. Seventy-one people lost their lives.[3]

An inquiry following the failure of the building structure found the owner guilty of faulty construction. He was arrested.[4] But that did little to address the ten thousand or so similar buildings in the same region on shaky foundations and unstable sand. Those who live there do so at their own risk. Weak foundations built on ground of questionable reliability have left area residents vulnerable.

"I take a longer route to go to market but I do not use the alley next to this building because it might cave in any day," said a neighbor interviewed by *Times of India*.[5]

If you are wondering why so many buildings were built on such unstable ground, look no further than greed itself. "No one bothers to follow structural safety norms. Here, houses are constructed very fast because the owners want to rent them out quickly. Most owners seem to ignore the building guidelines," said Lalita Park secretary Sushil Kamur.[6]

"The lure of the money is the real problem" is the way local official Shakil Saifi summed it up.[7]

Foundations matter. The ground on which you build matters. I know that firsthand having lived in Texas for so long. The Texas heat has a way of drying out the ground completely. It is notorious for causing even the best-built foundations to shift over time. A number of years ago, I saw the results of this show up on my bedroom wall.

At first, Lois and I noticed a few seemingly harmless cracks appear on the wall. Before long, those cracks gave birth to more cracks, and we had what looked like a map of cracks crisscrossing in the paint. So I did what anyone would do—I called a painter to repair the plaster.

The painter came. He stripped the old plaster. Added some new plaster. Repainted it. I paid him. He was happy. I was happy. Lois was happy. All seemed well.

But around a month later, Lois turned to me and said, "Tony, are those new cracks on our wall?"

Surely not, I thought. But looking more closely, I saw that she was right. More cracks had appeared on the new plaster and paint. So I did what anyone would do—I called the painter back and asked him to come fix the work he had done. He obviously had done it wrong.

The painter came. He took off his now-cracked plaster. Added some new plaster. Repainted it. I didn't pay him this time. He wasn't that happy. I wasn't that happy either. But all seemed well.

A couple of months passed, and this time when new cracks appeared, it looked as though they had brought all of their aunts, uncles, and cousins along too. Now I had a family of cracks on my bedroom wall. Obviously, I needed a different painter. So I did what anyone would do—I called a new painter because the previous guy just wasn't getting the job done.

The new painter came. He looked at the cracks on my wall, then he looked at me. He ran his hands along the cracks on my wall, then he looked again at me. He continued to stare at the cracks on my wall rather than getting out his tool to scrape off the plaster. I looked at him.

Finally, after what seemed like an inordinate amount of time, he turned to me and said, "I'm sorry, Tony. I can't help you."

I stared at him, somewhat surprised, and asked, "But isn't this what you do?"

He responded quickly, "Oh yes, this is what I do. I'm a painter. But I can't help you."

"Why can't you help me?" I asked, running out of options.

"Because you don't have a problem with the cracks on your wall," he responded.

I looked at the cracks on my wall, which I supposedly was not having any problems with, then I looked at him.

"Hold on," I stated. "I see a crack. You see a crack. The fact of the matter is that all God's children see a crack! There are cracks on my wall!" My tone carried with it a bit of superiority mixed with frustration, I'll admit. I was now officially evangelically ticked off. My new painter, trying to calm my concern, went on to explain, "Oh yes, there are cracks on your wall. The cracks are real. I'm not saying they aren't real. I'm just saying that those cracks are not your problem."

I looked at him as if to say he should continue without my asking. He stood there instead. So I asked, attempting to remain patient by voicing each word slowly, "Then what's my problem?"

"Your problem is that you have a shifting foundation under your house," he replied. "Your foundation is moving. What you're seeing on your wall is just a symptom of a much deeper problem." He then paused like a painter waiting for the first coat to dry before adding the next in order to let what he had said sink in. "Until you solidify your foundation," he continued, "you will always be doing patchwork on your wall."

Men, today there are a lot of cracks all around us. Cracks in our lives. Cracks in our families. Cracks with our kids. There are cracks in our direction, economics, relationships, politics, and careers. There are also racial cracks. Class cracks. And, of course, crack cracks. Cracks have broken out everywhere around and among us. As a result, we spend a great amount of our time, money, and energy trying to patch up the cracks to make things look better. For a while they do look better. But before long we discover that, given enough time, the cracks reappear.

This is because the foundation keeps moving. The foundation has not been solidified. Any structure that stands on a weak foundation will have cracks in its walls. Any life standing on the same will become rife with its own brokenness as well.

This isn't new information. Every athlete knows that to be successful you have to strengthen the core. The core, your foundation, controls your ability for movement. A stronger core allows for greater balance, reach, and overall performance. Similarly, a stronger spiritual foundation enables a successful life. Foundations aren't fancy, and foundations aren't pretty, but they had better be solid.

Jesus told us this in His tale of two men.

> Therefore everyone who hears these words of Mine and acts on them, may be compared to a wise man who built his house on the rock. And the rain fell, and the floods came, and the winds blew and slammed against that house; and yet it did not fall, for it had been founded on the rock. Everyone who hears these words of Mine and does not act on them, will be like a foolish man who built his house on the sand. The rain fell, and the floods came, and the winds blew and slammed against that house; and it fell—and great was its fall.
>
> Matthew 7:24–27

In this parable, one house stood against the storm. The other house fell. Not only did it fall, but Jesus emphasized that "great was its fall." It didn't just topple over. No, this house came crashing down, most likely destroying everything and everyone in its proximity.

Same storm. Different results. But why?

A look at the lives and choices of these two men will give us the answer. It will also give us insight into what it means to be a kingdom man rising high. After all, you can't build a skyscraper on the foundation of a chicken coop. The higher you plan to build, the deeper and wider your foundation must be. Our problem today is that we have too many men aiming high without the necessary spiritual foundation to maintain their dreams. One wrong move, and the whole thing tumbles down like a badly balanced Jenga game.

Men, you are the foundation. It's all banking on you. Thus, in this day of male abandonment, male abuse, male disregard, and male irresponsibility, we have cultural chaos. God declares clearly that men have the primary responsibility of establishing the foundation for all else.

Individual, Family, Church, and Society Influence

For starters, these two men in Jesus' parable had some common traits and values. They were on the same page when it came to dreaming. Both wanted to build a house. Both had a vision for constructing something in which to live.

Now, before we go further it's important to note that in Scripture, a house can symbolically refer to one of four different things. A house can refer to someone's personal life, as is implied in this story. Both men wanted a life of substance, significance, and status. They wanted to accomplish something. In short, they wanted a life that mattered. They didn't want to just pass their days on earth and have nothing to show for it.

> **Individual**: Kingdom men pursue their personal purpose and aim to leave a lasting impact.

Also, a house in the Bible can refer to building a family. Families are frequently referenced in Scripture as the "house of" a certain person. We read about the "house of David" (Isaiah 22:22) or the "house of Isaac" (Amos 7:16). Likewise, no serious kingdom man walks down the aisle to get married all the while planning to get divorced. No kingdom man should be planning on abandoning his children.

Family: Kingdom men seek to impact their homes in such a way that all within them grow to be mature, responsible believers in Christ.

Thirdly, building a house in the Bible can refer to building a ministry. The temple in the Old Testament was sometimes called the house of God (see Exodus 34:26). The church in the New Testament is called the "household of the faith" (Galatians 6:10). And Jesus referred to the temple as the "house of prayer" (Matthew 21:13). The concept of a house is often tied to spiritually based cultural influence.

Church: Kingdom men concern themselves with the spiritual footprint they are making with their lives.

Lastly, building a house can signify a focus on building a society. After all, Israel was called the "house of Israel." In our contemporary history, we speak of societal rule as taking place in the White House or in the House of Representatives. The house denotes that which is to represent and oversee society. Thus, to build a house is also to build a community that is whole and unified and that benefits the citizenry.

Society: Kingdom men involve themselves in the structural entities that govern a land so as to influence the culture for Christ.

Both of these men in Jesus' parable dreamed of building a house. Therefore, both men housed within their own hearts a desire for personal development, familial influence, ministry impact, and societal good. They wanted a life of significance. A family that was strong. A ministry that was effective. And a culture that was ordered well. Kingdom men desire nothing less.

The second thing these two men had in common was that they lived in the same neighborhood. We know this because they were affected by the same storm. The passage tells us that the rain fell and the floods came and the wind hit both of their homes.

For context, a storm in Scripture refers to an adverse set of circumstances. When the Bible speaks of a storm, the writer is conveying negative events entering into a life. A storm connotes trouble, tribulation, and trials. Storms seek to knock you over—mentally, emotionally, physically, and spiritually. You are either in a storm, just heading out of a storm, or about to experience a storm. This is because life is full of troubles (John 16:33). That's just the way it is, and I wouldn't be doing my job as a teacher of truth if I told you otherwise.

I would love to write a book, or even a chapter, and tell you that following Jesus means it will never rain. It would be great to preach a sermon titled "No Storms for Those Following the Savior." But I'd be lying. Storms tear through towns, and frequently at that. It's going to rain, thunder, and hail. On everyone.

The other day I went to my mailbox and pulled out the mail. Looking at the top piece I noticed that it merely was addressed "Occupant." Translation: "We don't care who lives here—we're just trying to sell you something." Last I checked, storms don't sell anything, but they similarly don't care who lives in their destructive path. They don't care how much you earn or even what you do. Hail is hail, and it will dent any car it comes into contact with. Wind is wind, and it will destroy any building its tornadic forces push against. Rain is rain, and when it floods it doesn't ask your permission or level of prominence first.

Storms affect us all. Just as they affected these two men's shared vision of a brighter tomorrow. Both men wanted to build a house, along with all that the house represented. But they went about it in two very different ways.

The third thing the men shared is that they were listening to the same biblical truth. Since Jesus, the living Word, was proclaiming the written Word, they were equally exposed to divine revelation. So they were not being influenced by contradicting information.

Two Options: You Choose

The difference between the men's approaches is told to us in Matthew 7:24 and 26. Let's look at those two verses again:

A wise man . . . built his house on the rock.

A foolish man . . . built his house on the sand.

Did you catch where the difference showed up? At the foundation. The wise man chose solid ground on which to build. The foolish man built his house on the sand. These men chose drastically different foundations upon which to construct the buildings of their dreams, winding up with drastically different results.

The structure is never where you start. You don't put up the doors first and frame the windows. You always start with the foundation because everything else stands on its stability. The ability of everything to hold steady in the midst of a storm rests squarely on the strength of the foundation.

So why would the foolish man build on sand? We gain a clue by what we read earlier about the houses going up near the Yamuna River. We read that the builders built quickly and cheaply in order to get a greater profit. The fool in this tale of two men did the same. Building on sand is going to be quick because you are not digging down through hard earth or rock. It doesn't take long to create a sandcastle of sorts. But when you build on rock, it requires excavating, moving, and more. All of that increases both time and cost.

One man was willing to put in the time and the extra expense to build on a solid foundation. The other man wasn't. He let greed lay the groundwork, getting his home up fast and without much cost. Unfortunately for him, it came down about as fast as it had gone up. If not faster.

The tale of these two men from long ago reflects a cacophony of questions many of us are asking today as well. What does it mean to build a life on a solid foundation? How do I create something lasting? How can I keep it from crashing down? When is the storm coming? How strong are the winds? Should I build high? Is it better to build wide? Should I go this direction or that? This career or that one? Work this many hours, or that many? Questions like these pummel men's minds like pellets of hail in a hot summer storm. The rat race has us all running on a wheel at times. But Jesus gives us the answer to all of this and more when He tells us how we can each choose to live as the wise man or the fool. It's simple:

> Therefore everyone who hears these words of Mine and acts on them, may be compared to a wise man.
>
> v. 24

Everyone who hears these words of Mine and does not act on them, will be like a foolish man.

v. 26

For starters, Jesus is assuming one thing. He's assuming you're hearing His words. But hearing is never solely the answer. A running back might hear the play called that requires him to rush behind the quarterback to grab the ball. He might hear it clearly. But if he doesn't do it—if he fails to execute the play—the play is most likely over. It's never in the hearing alone. It's always in the doing that makes a man great (see James 1:22).

The difference between a strong foundation and a weak one is not merely information. You can have a PhD in information but still be a fool. The difference lies in whether you know how and are willing to apply the information you heard. That's wisdom.

God's Word does not work just because you get excited about it when you read it. It doesn't work just because you heard a sermon or a podcast and got all fired up. It doesn't even work because you spent some time thinking about it or posted a verse on social media. That's all nice. But if it's not applied, you won't get to experience the full manifestation of what it is meant to do in your life. To listen to God's Word but refuse to act on it causes a man to do little more than waste his life.

When God did spectacular things in the Bible, He always required the people He was working through to do something first. He told Moses to hold out his rod. When Moses did, then He opened the Red Sea. He told Joshua to have the priests step into the water. When the priests did, then God held the flooding river back. Jesus told those at the tomb of Lazarus to move the stone. When they did, then He raised Lazarus from the dead. He told the disciples to bring what they could find to eat. When they did, then He fed five thousand with some crackers and sardines (five loaves and two fish). Over and over again God would tell a person, or a group of people, to do something that would then activate the power of His Word.

The reason a lot of men are not seeing God move miraculously in their lives is that God is not seeing them move in an act of faith. By the way, attending church does not count as an act of faith. Simply hearing the Word will never produce the supernatural intervention of God in your circumstances. Until He detects obedience and alignment to what He said, you're pretty much on your own. God's authority to overcome obstacles or move you forward in your dreams is activated by action, not talk.

Wisdom is both the ability and the responsibility of applying God's truth to life's choices. You can only identify a wise man or a fool by his decisions. Not by the songs he sings in church. Not by the Scriptures he quotes either. Many men know how to speak fluent Christianese. But all that means absolutely nothing unless you are seeking outcomes through aligning spiritual truths with life's scenarios. Biblical wisdom is about as practical a thing as you can get. It's always tied to the day-in and day-out decisions based on what a person thinks, says, and does. When you choose God by your actions, you activate the divine programming from the Word to go to work for you in bringing about good results.

> When you choose God by your actions, you activate the divine programming from the Word to go to work for you in bringing about good results.

Unfortunately, too many men try to mix rock with sand. They'll apply a bit of truth along with a bit of a lie. Yet mixing rock and sand only produces sandy rock. It's not solid either. It's what we know as "human wisdom." It's man's point of view. This is often based on what your parents or the school system taught you, what your friends say, or even what the media might say. But any time you add sand to rock, you get the same disastrous result as you would if you added a bit of arsenic to your stew. When you do this, Matthew 15:6 says you literally have canceled out the power of God's Word: "You invalidated the word of God for the sake of your tradition." When you bring man's point of view and attach it to God, and when it contradicts God's point of view, you cancel out God's. Thus, you also cancel out His strength and divine intervention in your life.

So a lot of us actually cancel out the very thing we need most. We cancel it out by bringing an antithesis into the equation. Scripture says,

"Let God be found true, though every man be found a liar" (Romans 3:4). When God says *A* and you think *B*, God is saying, "Don't merge your *B* with my *A*." When you disagree with God, the conversation you need to have is with you, not Him. You need to tell yourself, "Self, you're lying to me right now, because God says this and so this is true."

The fastest way to neuter your call to greatness as a kingdom man is through double-mindedness. James 1:7–8 couldn't be more clear: "That person should not expect to receive anything from the Lord. Such a person is double-minded and unstable in all they do" (NIV). In other words, let the double-minded man know he will get nothing. Bringing human wisdom into divine revelation in order to make your own choices removes God's involvement. Once you merge the two views through double-mindedness, God steps back. You're on your own. In fact, a lot of men are actually canceling their own prayers. They are negating the effectiveness of their prayers by making choices built on the sandy soil of human thought.

This reminds me of a challenge I faced in learning to ride horses. Lois and I had taken the kids to Pine Cove Camp in eastern Texas and we were excited about riding the horses. I figured that I knew what to do. I'd seen enough Westerns like *Gunsmoke*, *Rawhide*, and *Bonanza*. I'd seen them all. So I got on the horse and made the *click, click* sound with my mouth, then said, "Hai, giddyap!" and pressed in with my heels.

The problem is I had an afflicted horse. This horse was going nowhere. Each time I kicked it, my horse would take a few steps back and then a few steps forward. So I called the wrangler over to request a new horse because obviously it had to be the horse's fault. I'd seen more than enough Westerns to know that's not what horses are supposed to do. But the wrangler just smiled and explained, "This horse isn't crazy, Tony."

He patted the horse and then looked toward me again. "You can't just say, 'Giddyap' and kick it at the same time you are pulling back on the reins. You're confusing the horse. He doesn't know if you want him to go forward or backward, so he's doing both."

Relatedly, a lot of men come to church or read the Bible or attend a small group—even lead it—and say, "Giddyap, King Jesus. Ride on!" at the same time as pulling back on the reins with human thought. They then wonder why things aren't going anywhere in their lives. It's because you can't merge fact with fiction and wind up with a foundation built on the solid stability of truth. Your foundation will collapse when the storms rage or the typhoon rolls through town, inflicting damage on anyone and everyone around. And even if you do avoid a strong storm or two, your weak foundation will show up in other ways.

Early on in our marriage, Lois and I took a trip to Italy and stopped at the Tower of Pisa. It wasn't much to look at, to be honest. Just a short tower leaning, and a lot of people leaning as well as they gazed or took some touristy photos. That's it. I wasn't impressed. We did learn, though, that it is predicted this tower will eventually collapse unless a way is found to correct the continual progression of the lean.

We also discovered why the tower leans. The reason is found in the meaning of the name of the town itself. *Pisa* means "marshy." This tower was built on a shallow foundation of sand, clay, and marshy dirt. Due to wars and military conflicts, this tower took over two hundred years to build, and it's been leaning ever since. The city is home to many towers, not quite as tall or as famous, that also suffer from foundational instabilities. Sandy soil will do that. It will leave you with uninhabitable buildings only fit for a photo.

God created you for more than to just be a photo on a social media site. He has a purpose for you. He has a dream for you to live out. But in order to awaken to your full potential, you have to start on a solid foundation. That means more than just knowing, studying, or memorizing His Word. You have to act on it. The power of His promises remains dormant unless activated by your faith through what you do. Your foundation determines your future.

Your foundation is the Word of God *applied*. It's not just the Word of God *known*. You will not see the intervention of God until He sees your obedience to His truth. God is waiting on you to take your rightful place in this world. He is waiting for you to rise to the occasion and secure your spot of significance in His kingdom made manifest on earth. But that only happens when you step out—fully, faithfully, and single-mindedly—according to the direction of His will.

Now, I'm not suggesting following God will keep you from the storm. Sometimes if you follow Him, like the disciples who sailed straight into the monstrous storm on the Sea of Galilee, He will direct you into the eye of the storm. But what I am saying is that when you choose to live by His truth, you will engage the programming of His Word and witness His work in the midst of the storm. The wise man in our tale of two men still faced the storm. He didn't avoid the hurricane that came his way. He just withstood it. He didn't succumb to it, because he had built his life on the right foundation.

When I was a boy growing up in Baltimore, my dad got me an inflatable punching bag for Christmas one year. I loved this punching bag. Every time I hit it, it would immediately drop to the floor. But then, just as quickly, it bounced back. This feature allowed me to hit it time and time again, as many times as I wanted. Each time I boxed that punching bag with my full strength, it just hit the ground and bounced right back up.

> God is waiting for you to rise to the occasion and secure your spot of significance in His kingdom made manifest on earth.

One time I thought I'd be clever and kick the bag. I just wanted to see what would happen. As you might imagine, the punching bag went flying across the room. First it hit the wall, then it hit the ceiling, but then it came back to the ground. And after some wobbling around, it went back to its upright position. No matter what I did to this punching bag, it always came back up with that knowing smile painted on its face. It's almost like the smile taunted me to try to keep it knocked down!

But the reason it would never stay down despite all my efforts was because there was a weight at the bottom of the bag that was heavier than the top. This foundational weight caused the bag to right itself after withstanding whatever I did to it.

I wish I could close out this chapter by telling you that trouble will never come your way. But I wouldn't be telling the truth. This world is fallen. We live in a sin-stained atmosphere that affects us all. You might get hit. You might get knocked down—more than once. Satan has a pretty nasty right hook. But what I can tell you, despite all of that, is if you build your life on the solid foundation of applying God's Word to your decisions, you will bounce back up. You will overcome. You will hold your head high. You will smile. Sure, it might look crooked after enough hits, but that's okay. Because when all hell breaks loose, and it does sometimes—I know this firsthand—if you are resting on the right foundation, you will stand strong.

FOUR

THE SECRET TO SUCCESS

I stood surrounded by towering trees whose lives reached further back into history than my own. Nearly two hundred acres of sprawling hillsides, creeks, and magnificently manicured greens stretched out before me like pristinely placed oil on canvas. The picture aroused emotions of awe, to say the least. It was as if I had stepped into another land in a different time.

As I stood there, the chaos, fear, and uncertainty that plagued our culture during the onset of the coronavirus pandemic faded away into nothing. The doubts, noise, and "world-is-ending" chatter drifted into the clear blue skies, as if absorbed by the atmosphere itself.

Here, there was peace. No fear. No need for clever maneuvers or quick sideways turns to create social distancing either. The nearly 160 acres provided plenty of space for those of us who were there. No one had to dodge anyone else. Now, that's not to say no one had to dodge any balls.

We all went about our activities enjoying the renewed energy that comes from experiencing nature, good company, and a great game of golf.

That I was standing fewer than ten miles from the heart of downtown Dallas never crossed my mind. The construction, noise, and cultural clashes of the city didn't have any effect here. Here, things were calm. Positive. Prosperous. Powerful. I breathed it all in deeply. I needed a break from the constant demands the crisis had placed on me.

Even though I am not a golfer, my emotions would soon board a roller coaster of sorts as I hopped into a cart to set out across the horizon. First, I felt great satisfaction knowing the seed God had placed in my spirit nearly twenty years ago now thrived in front of my eyes. I felt a sense of wholeness in taking in the reality that something I had prayed for and asked God to provide had been supplied. We had finally purchased the Golf Club of Dallas as a business development enterprise to keep the community strong around the church, a dream I had held for so long. I also felt dignity, recognizing the rule of racism no longer had its grip on this place.

The last course designed by Perry Maxwell before his death, and completed by his son Press in the early 1950s, this course carries a harsh history. The stunning, well-kept grounds lined with flowing streams and bridges underneath a canopy of green drew a lot of attention in that day. Carefully designed holes quickly garnered the applause of golf enthusiasts around the nation as it hosted the Byron Nelson Classic on the PGA Tour for many years.

As I mentioned, this visit was during the early stages of the global COVID-19 pandemic. Many of the private golf courses in the heart of Dallas had remained closed even after Dallas County lifted the shelter-in-place order for golf courses as "essential outdoor activities." But this course reopened and, as a result, had numbers of individuals enjoying exercise, fellowship, and sunshine while remaining strategically spaced apart.

I quickly noticed as I drove that nearly everyone I saw on the course was white. This could have been due to the other courses in Dallas remaining closed a bit longer, meaning people who wouldn't normally come to this course had driven in. This club typically sees more diversity. But on this day, I was pretty much the entirety of ethnic diversity when it came to racial representation. It painted a picture that led to a memory of a painful past.

It reminded me of when Lois and I had moved close to this course more than three decades ago. We had moved into our modest home in South Dallas at a time when African Americans were not allowed to play on the course. While we could see the greens from our front door, we knew we couldn't step on them. We certainly couldn't eat at the restaurant or host an event in the ornate clubhouse either. In fact, it wouldn't be until nearly 1990 that this course would admit its first black member.[1] Yes, I did say 1990.

Granted, 1990 was a lot earlier than the Dallas Country Club up north. They didn't open up their membership until 2014. And even when they did, they issued a statement that read more like a condition to some. The president, Ray Nixon, had this to say of the African American they admitted as a new member, describing him as "an outstanding individual and friend."[2] It's almost as if there was a felt need to vouch for him. I'm not sure other members needed labels declaring them "outstanding" upon their entrance. But such is the context of the culture at hand.

Due to the intrinsic nature of racism and the overarching effect it leaves on those caught in its web, it was difficult not to revisit those thoughts as I drove the course that morning. My emotions soon followed suit, like a perfectly hit ball heading for the hole. What had previously been high feelings of satisfaction and success now dropped down into the dark shadows of sadness. Instantly I felt raw. Broken. Alone. And even disappointed.

Tears formed first in my heart and then threatened my eyes. How many times had Lois and I prayed about one day purchasing this golf course for the community and economic development strategy of the ministry? This profitable course was slated to earn back the investment in just a few short years, enabling us to invest profits in future outreaches such as our dream for a health center aimed specifically at addressing minority health risks and needs.

Lois knew that I would often go sit on the steps of our church's Christian Education Center, which was just several feet from the fence of the course. I would look out over the land and pray, asking God to make it ours. I must have gone there to pray over a hundred times in the last decade. My vision of preserving urban areas as a model for community development nationwide had come true in many aspects and on many acres, but this course had always been an elusive part of that plan. Until now.

I recalled those conversations Lois and I had, talking about how we believed God would make this a reality someday. We would smile at the thought that a golf course that had once denied black participation entirely would be owned by a black-run ministry. I thought about how Lois had urged me to move forward in getting this course just a few weeks before she passed away. With very little strength by that time, she'd said, "Tony, God told me you should move forward on this acquisition."

Now, as I drove around in the cart alone, I remembered that moment. I remembered her enthusiasm and her tears when she said it. And my heart sank. I wanted her with me to experience this. I wanted her to see this. I wanted her to celebrate what God had done in turning what once felt to me like a societal disgrace into a spiritual success.

But God didn't plan things that way. And it was up to me to accept that. To work through the grief, yes, but also to accept that in this life you can have joy and sorrow simultaneously. In fact, this is often the case.

> Spiritual success often requires development, spiritual battles, maturing, and wilderness seasons along the way.

Especially in times of success. Many times, true spiritual success comes underscored with a proviso of life's pain. This is because spiritual success often requires development, spiritual battles, maturing, and wilderness seasons along the way.

The reason I bring this critical aspect up is because I feel that many men do not envision success as it really is. They envision it all culminating in fireworks, glitz, and one big resounding stadium of applause. Unfortunately, this expectation causes these men to miss success when it comes along. As a result of not recognizing it, they wind up chasing the next big thing. And then the next.

Many of the milestones of success in our lives may actually be bittersweet, when all is said and done. That's because we live in a broken world tainted by sin and its effects. But unless we realize what true success looks like and recognize what spiritual success is, we may wind up on a never-ending quest for something we've already obtained in many ways.

Defining Success

Before we go any further, let me define success. Spiritually, success is fulfilling God's purpose for your life. The biblical definition of success means living out your God-given purpose. In our culture today, there are a number of errant descriptions of what it means to be successful. Some people assume that success comes tied to how much money a person has. Others base it on how high up the career ladder you go. More and more these days, success is defined by how many followers you have on social media or how many likes you get. But the problem with all these assumptions is that they are not based on God's standard of success.

Jesus gave us the definition of success when He said to His father, "I glorified You on the earth, having accomplished the work which You have given Me to do" (John 17:4).

Paul said the same thing in a different way when he penned these words: "I have fought the good fight, I have finished the course, I have kept the faith" (2 Timothy 4:7).

In fact, God told Joshua that his success was entirely based on his careful meditation on the Word of God combined with aligning his decisions and actions underneath it (Joshua 1:8). Success involves fulfilling what God has called you to do.

Everyone wants to be a success. Nobody sets out to fail. And while none of us can go back and undo the mistakes of yesteryears, each of us has the option of becoming successful from here on out. We can either begin the journey or continue the journey of fulfilling God's destiny for us as kingdom men.

God gives us the secret to living a life of success in Psalm 25:14 when He shares with us through David, "The secret of the LORD is for those who fear Him, and He will make them know His covenant." To know God's covenant is to know His favor and His blessings, as God's covenant is expressly tied to His covering. Align yourself underneath God's relational covenantal rule in life and you will experience spiritual success. But there is a condition to success, this secret reveals. You only get to know God's covenant by fearing God. There exists a cause-and-effect scenario for achieving spiritual success.

Let me change Psalm 25:14 by reversing its order to make it more clear:

If you do not fear God, you won't get the secrets of the covenant.

Fearing God leads to knowing the secrets of the covenant. The secrets of the covenant lead to spiritual success. If you don't fear God, the path to personal success will remain a secret. But unlocking this secret gives you access to the covenant—it is like unlocking a door to a treasure.

A covenant is a spiritually binding relationship ordained by God through which He advances His kingdom. It's the mechanism through which He accomplishes His purposes, goals, and agenda. It's an arrangement of a relationship, not merely an official contract.

If you're married, you know what it's like to have secrets that you share only with your spouse. Other people have general things to discuss with you, but as a couple, you often share your innermost hopes and thoughts with each other. These are the hidden things accessible by the nature of the covenantal relationship of marriage. In fact, secrets are often so valued and guarded that they are spoken in whispers. You need to be close, not only relationally but often physically, in order to share secrets.

Men, accessing God's covenant through fearing Him lets you in on His secrets. It brings you close enough to God to hear Him whisper. God unveils His purposes and promises for your life when you are in close proximity to Him.

In football, everything is measured by the location of the ball. A first down starts where the ball has been placed. A touchdown depends on whether the ball crosses the plane of the goal line. A field goal is when the ball goes between the two posts. A reception occurs if the receiver catches the ball. If the receiver bobbles the ball and then drops it, the team heads back to where the ball had been placed at the start of that play. Everything is measured by the presence of and relationship to the football. That reality determines everything that happens in the game, especially the outcome of the game.

Similarly, your relationship to the covenant will determine how much of God you experience, or how little. It will determine how far and how fast you move forward in life. It will determine whether you score or whether you have to keep punting the ball to someone else. Most importantly, it will determine your level of success—whether you win or lose. Your level of success is all about your connection to the covenant.

Often when I travel for ministry, my son Jonathan comes with me. Because I've flown with American Airlines for so many years, I have earned the privilege of upgrading to first class for free when there are seats available. Not only that, but American Airlines makes this benefit available to the person traveling with me as well. It's called a "companion upgrade." A former standout football player and not exactly small in stature, Jonathan appreciates this! By virtue of his relationship with me, he gets plenty of legroom on the plane.

But we ran into a problem on a recent trip when I went up to the counter to check on our upgrades. I was able to upgrade my seat, but Jonathan was not. I explained to the lady behind the counter that he was my son, traveling with me. But she promptly told me it didn't matter if he was flying with me because he didn't get ticketed with me. On this particular trip, Jonathan had been ticketed at a different time. A companion upgrade only works when the tickets are purchased and processed together.

I stood there surprised. After all, he is my son. I tried that approach again, but she just as quickly replied that even though he may be my son legally, he is not my companion relationally on this particular trip. Thus, he was not entitled to what I had in the way of upgrades. Because Jonathan wasn't linked with me, he wound up back in coach, uncomfortable at best.

Men, you may have accepted Jesus Christ as your personal Savior, and you may have become a son of the King through a spiritual rebirth. But if you are not connected by the relationship of the covenant, through the fear of God, you don't get the upgrade to receive all of the benefits. The secret to success is available through a connection called sanctification, not merely through the legal justification. Yes, you are still on your way to heaven by virtue of your new birth as a child of the King. But unless you are intimately connected with God relationally, on the same page covenantally through fearing Him, you forfeit the upgrade. When that curtain closes behind the good-smelling food in first class, you'll be stuck in coach with the rest.

Without the connection to the covenant, the curtain remains closed just as firmly as any door with a lock. God is looking to see whether you take Him seriously before handing out a key. It is the fear of the Lord that gives you the privilege and right to access the blessings behind the door.

Treasures of Many Kinds

So that raises a question: What are the blessings behind the door? What's lurking there that is so penetrating and substantive we would want to pursue it? We get a peek at what lies there for each of us in Isaiah 33:6: "And He will be the stability of your times, a wealth of salvation, wisdom and knowledge; the fear of the Lord is his treasure."

Fearing God gives you full access to nothing less than treasure itself. In fact, we see in the verse we just looked at that there are treasures of many kinds. For one, it "will be the stability of your times." This treasure will offer you strength when things should be shaky. It will also give you provision in seasons of drought. In the treasure of God's covenant, you have all you need to get through trying times.

I can tell you firsthand that I understand what it means to have God himself as my stability. In the months following the loss of my life partner in marriage, Lois, I didn't always know which way was up. One time in particular, I walked into our home after being at the office all day and broke down sobbing as soon as I crossed the threshold. The busy schedule of the day had allowed me some respite from my grief through distraction. But when I got home, Lois's absence came crashing down on me like a ton of bricks, collapsing me into emotions filled with loneliness and loss. I wept for what was probably minutes but seemed like hours. I missed her. I missed her smile and the sound of her voice greeting me as she had done for the nearly five full decades of our time together.

And yet in the middle of all these emotions and struggles each day—I had many days when I didn't want to get out of bed—I leaned on God for His strength. And He gave it without fail. Let me give you an example. On my first solo trip to film a Bible study after Lois had transitioned, tears threatened to come down my face as I walked the corridor of the airport alone. We had gone on these Bible study production trips together in the past. It was a great way for me to work while we still got to be together and see God's beautiful nature in various places.

But this trip was different. Lois had gone on to be with the Lord only six weeks prior. I agreed to go on the trip to film the study because I knew that God would meet me along the way and that healing comes through times of searching, not just times of sulking. Yet as I walked alone this very first time, luggage in hand, tears rose up in my soul. I sighed. But God met me right there as only He could.

It just so happened that a couple at the airport, whom I did not know, recognized me and came over to introduce themselves and say hello. They had heard about Lois's passing and they said they just wanted to give me a hug. This was before the coronavirus, when hugs were still a thing! They also said they felt God telling them to pray for me. So right there in the airport, they prayed.

I could feel God's Spirit lifting my heart and my mind up out of the pit I had sunk into. By the time they were finished praying, I had regained my strength. Nothing else had changed. It was still my first solo trip to film a Bible study without my lovemate alongside. But despite the challenges ahead, God was reminding me that He knew just how to get me through it. And He did.

Men, God can get you through whatever you are facing too. But first He needs you to wake up from the slumber of self in order to proactively pursue an intimate relationship with Him. That awakening of biblical manhood can only take place when you learn to fear God. Which brings us to an important question: *What does it mean to fear God?* I touched on this some in my book *Kingdom Man*, but I want to give a foundational reminder here since much of our success as men rests on this principle.

Power Under Control

I'm not going to give you a long, drawn-out theological definition that might sound nice but leaves little in the way of understanding. Rather, let me just talk to you man-to-man. I'll give you the bottom line: Fearing God means to take Him seriously.

To fear God merges two concepts. One involves being afraid of something, and the other is being in awe of it. Fearing God isn't one or the other. It's a convergence of both. When you mix these two together—being afraid and in awe—it translates into a life that takes God seriously. This is opposed to taking God casually, of course.

Unfortunately, many men take God casually. What they do is put a little icing on their religion and call it a day. They go to church. Hold their Bible. Say their public prayers. Do devotions. They cross off that checklist of so-called "spiritual" items so it will appear they are taking God seriously. They may convince others that they are taking God seriously. But God never looks from the outside in. God looks at your heart (1 Samuel 16:7). A man who fears God understands this. A kingdom man realizes that God is not tricked. He is to be honored from the heart. Authentically honoring God comes through aligning our decisions under His comprehensive rule.

Another way to illustrate the combination of fear and awe comes in something we all do—drive. Driving has become a normal way of getting around. But did you ever stop to think of the power that is found in a car? Without going into the minutia of physics, let me give a fairly simple example. It's been stated that if you crash your car while driving at 65 miles per hour, it is the same force you would face if you drove your car off a twelve-story building.[3]

Now, most of us driving a car on top of a twelve-story building would be extremely careful. Yet many of us casually driving down the road at 65 miles per hour have been known to let our minds wander. The reason we pay more attention on top of the building is that we can see the potential result should we drive off the edge. Resultantly, we take our driving up there seriously. But since we have become so used to driving on highways at 65 miles per hour, many of us don't consider how dangerous it really is. Car accidents are the eighth leading cause of death globally, topped only by serious health-related issues.[4] What's more, it's cited that up to 50 percent of accidents are due to distracted driving.[5] Essentially, they are due to people not taking driving seriously. Messing around while driving isn't a game that should be played. As soon as you take your attention off the road, where it needs to be, a crash can loudly declare, "Game over."

In other words, there are boundaries around the use of a high-powered vehicle. And those boundaries are honored through what we do. In fact, we even tell our kids and grandkids when they are old enough to drive that they are to honor those boundaries. We take driving seriously.

Yet far too many men understand how to take driving seriously but have no clue how to do the same with God. They want the benefits of God without the boundaries that a proper fear and awe of Him create. They treat God like the cop they see in the rearview mirror. He affects what you do when He's in visible proximity—perhaps in church or a small-group setting. But get outside of cultural Christianity, and the foot presses hard on the accelerator once again.

It's easy to fear God when you're in church, affected by His presence. The singing, preaching, and fellowship all contribute to a culture of reverence. But when you go out into your day-to-day world, it can get more difficult. It seems then that many men are no longer impacted by God's perspective. Life goes on as usual, with just a visit to God every once in a while.

Fearing God involves more than feelings brought on by a quick visit. Sure, feelings can be good and can come up during a Sunday morning service or while reading a great book. But feelings are not the measure of a man's commitment. The measure of a man's heart is revealed through what he does. A kingdom man demonstrates with his feet that he fears God. Fearing God involves your movement, not just your emotions.

No matter how much a child of yours tells you that he or she loves you, if they do the opposite of what you ask them to do, they aren't truly demonstrating that love. They aren't honoring you by taking your words and wishes seriously. They may have the emotion of a form of love, but they also have the actions of rebellion.

> Fearing God involves your movement, not just your emotions.

Many of God's children have the emotions of a form of love for God. They lift their hands and give the visible, physical reaction of loving God in particular settings. But when they make choices in their lives, they wind up moving in opposition to God's revealed will instead of toward it. In other words, they are living in rebellion.

What would you say to a basketball player who kept running toward the wrong basket while dribbling the ball? You'd probably tell him to go sit down. As a coach, you wouldn't have time for that.

Thankfully, God doesn't exist in time and He's not bound by linear limitations like we are. He's got all the time in the world, and then some. And He doesn't just kick us off the team for running in the wrong direction. God grasps that none of us is perfect and we all fall short (Romans 3:23). Yet that doesn't make our rebellion any less serious than it is. God's patience doesn't translate into a free pass to keep going with power out of control. God's patience translates into more time for us to grow.

Opening the Door

Rare is the man who jumps out of bed in the morning ready to take on the world. It typically takes a cup of coffee or some time to adjust from being fully asleep to fully awake. Likewise, as you awaken into biblical manhood, you want to look for spiritual growth and maturity that develops over time. It's a process that requires dedication and commitment. And as you grow by consistently applying God's Word to your decisions while depending on the Holy Spirit to empower those choices, there are three things you can come to expect in the treasure trove of the covenant:

Guidance

Prosperity

Legacy

We read about all three in Psalm 25:12–13, the two preceding verses to the one we looked at earlier in this chapter concerning the covenant.

> Who is the man who fears the LORD?
> He will instruct him in the way he should choose.
> His soul will abide in prosperity,
> And his descendants will inherit the land.

As you see, the first benefit you get as you awaken into biblical manhood through fearing the Lord is spiritual guidance. God himself will instruct you in the way you should go. It's hard to go wrong when you have divine instruction and direction.

Far too many of us are as spiritually lost as a jaybird. We don't know which way is up. We don't know how to make good decisions. A slew of bad decisions will catch up to you faster than wide receiver Tyreek Hill can race into an end zone. If you're constantly making wrong choices and then asking God to bless those wrong choices, you're going to wind up on the wrong path.

One of the greatest benefits of biblical manhood is that God will tell you the way you should go in order to live a life of success.

King David was a successful warrior even though he grew up herding sheep, skipping rocks, and playing instruments. David didn't attend military school. But he knew the one in charge. And because of that, David won his battles and his wars (see 1 Chronicles 18:1). A critical aspect of David's military leadership and victory came through his awareness of and willingness to seek God's guidance. No other biblical narrative contains more inquiries of God than David's. Each time he asked to know God's will and God's ways, he got an answer. We read it over and over again:

> So David inquired of the LORD, saying, "Shall I go and attack these Philistines?" And the LORD said to David, "Go and attack the Philistines and deliver Keilah."
>
> 1 Samuel 23:2

> Then David inquired of the LORD once more. And the LORD answered him and said, "Arise, go down to Keilah, for I will give the Philistines into your hand."
>
> 1 Samuel 23:4

> "Will the men of Keilah surrender me into his hand? Will Saul come down just as Your servant has heard? O LORD God of Israel, I pray, tell Your servant." And the LORD said, "He will come down."
>
> 1 Samuel 23:11

Then David said, "Will the men of Keilah surrender me and my men into the hand of Saul?" And the LORD said, "They will surrender you."

1 Samuel 23:12

David inquired of the LORD, saying, "Shall I pursue this band? Shall I overtake them?" And He said to him, "Pursue, for you will surely overtake them, and you will surely rescue all."

1 Samuel 30:8

Then it came about afterwards that David inquired of the LORD, saying, "Shall I go up to one of the cities of Judah?" And the LORD said to him, "Go up." So David said, "Where shall I go up?" And He said, "To Hebron."

2 Samuel 2:1

Then David inquired of the LORD, saying, "Shall I go up against the Philistines? Will You give them into my hand?" And the LORD said to David, "Go up, for I will certainly give the Philistines into your hand."

2 Samuel 5:19

When David inquired of the LORD, He said, "You shall not go directly up; circle around behind them and come at them in front of the balsam trees. It shall be, when you hear the sound of marching in the tops of the balsam trees, then you shall act promptly, for then the LORD will have gone out before you to strike the army of the Philistines."

2 Samuel 5:23–24

Now there was a famine in the days of David for three years, year after year; and David sought the presence of the LORD. And the LORD said, "It is for Saul and his bloody house, because he put the Gibeonites to death."

2 Samuel 21:1

Nine times David inquired of God. Nine times God gave him direction on what to do. As a result, David stood strongly positioned to annihilate his enemies and redeem his people from certain death. David, a kingdom man after God's own heart, understood the value of this treasure called guidance. He feared God, which enabled him to follow God more fully.

Life is full of choices. The problem with many of our decisions is that we cannot see what's around the bend. It's like being on a highway that is twisting and turning and you are unable to see around the next corner. You have to slow down because you don't know where you're going. Life is filled with unknowns.

But that's why David prayed a prayer we should all pray as kingdom men: "Make me know Your ways, O Lord; teach me Your paths" (Psalm 25:4). That's not just a sweet verse to say on Sunday. That's a plea for a game plan. It's a cry to know the next call. If you were a football player who had made it to the Super Bowl, would it make any sense to play it on your own? Would it make any sense to thank the coach for getting you there and then opt for your own schemes?

You don't need to answer either of those questions because both are rhetorical. Even so, we often do that with God. He begins opening doors for us and leading us to our destinies, and we just pat Him on the back and thank Him for getting us that far. "I'll take it from here, God," we say, as we walk toward our own plans and map out our own plays.

To know God's ways and for Him to show you His paths isn't about asking for more Scripture to memorize. It isn't about asking for another Bible study to take part in. David needed a personal answer for his situations and battles, each time, in order to win. Oftentimes, it was a matter of life and death—not only for David but for those under his care.

You and I need guidance from God as well. God's guidance helps us understand how to apply the wisdom of Scripture to our personal situations. It's about which way to go. What road should you take? Is there a better side street? Should you stop until things clear out ahead? God's guidance can get very specific when you're close enough to hear His voice.

In football, you have an NFL rulebook that comes from the league office in New York. It gives the rules of engagement for all thirty-two teams. It's the way it is and the way things will be. These rules don't adjust or change based on what city you are in or who your opponent happens to be. They are the standard by which the entire league seeks to operate.

It's the same standard for everyone. Teams don't get to make up certain rules for other teams.

But while there is only one rulebook, there are thirty-two different playbooks. This is because each team has its own plays. Each coach directs their team based on their playbook. Now, the playbook must be consistent with the rulebook and align under its rules, but it still can be unique to the team using it.

What's more, the maximization of the playbook is adjusted based on the opponent or even the progress of the game itself. The coach may have set out to play a certain style of game according to the team's playbook, but if his team falls behind quickly, he'll adjust. He'll adapt. He'll look at other aspects of his playbook and call different plays. Or at least, he should. This is because in a football game, as in life, things change. Expectations may get dashed. People can get hurt. The opponent might switch things up on you. Yet, regardless of the changes, a good strategic playbook will allow a team to adjust in order to seek the treasure of coming out on top.

God has given us a rulebook. It's His Word, and it sets the standard within which we, as kingdom men, are to play this game called life. But He also gives each of us our own playbook that we are free to tweak, adapt, and be guided by toward our own victory through the various twists and turns that take place. But you have to know the playbook and the rulebook to make the most of the game. The rulebook alone won't get you a *W* in the win column. Psalm 103:7 makes this distinction for us: "He [God] made known His *ways* to Moses, His *acts* to the sons of Israel" (emphasis added).

God gave Israel the rulebook (His acts). But He told Moses His plays (His ways). He whispered in his ear the way a friend whispers a secret. Why? Because Moses had a covenantal relationship with God based on intimacy and fellowship. It was not just based on a legal contract. Exodus 33:11 explains, "Thus the LORD used to speak to Moses face to face, just as a man speaks to his friend."

Do you want to know God's acts or His ways? Knowing God's *acts* means you become aware after the fact. It's already been done. But knowing God's *ways* means you get a glimpse of what is about to take place and why. This then informs how you respond as you go through it. It can also regulate your emotions, giving you a greater opportunity to see clearly and choose wisely. Taking God seriously opens the door for divine guidance particular to your specific situations in life. It's the first benefit of covenantal alignment.

Prospering as a Kingdom Man

The second benefit involves the prospering of your soul. We saw earlier in Psalm 25:13 that "his soul will abide in prosperity." Before you equate this to mean material gain, however, take a close look at what the passage says. It specifies that your "soul" will abide in prosperity. A person can have a lot of stuff but still have an impoverished soul. The soul is your life. It's your personhood. It's the emotions, mind, will, and consciousness of your being.

You can have a very big house with two miserable souls living in it. While the money may have multiplied for the individuals to purchase such a big house, it can't give wealth to the soul. God says if you fear Him, He will prosper your soul in such a way that it will impact everything you engage with. You'll be making wise decisions that will then affect your future success.

A kingdom man doesn't merely focus on the external things of life without making things better on the inside. But Satan has deceived so many of us into spending money we don't have in order to buy things we don't need so we can impress people we don't know. But all we wind up with are bills we can't pay. God's blessings work toward the well-being of the person. It's not about the stuff.

Before my grandson-in-law, Josh, married my granddaughter Kariss, he would come over with her to spend time with us at the house. One night when they stopped by, we talked about how a kingdom man manages his finances. Josh asked me a number of questions about planning for the future. I set out to give him God's blueprint for finances, explaining how a man oversees and manages his money.

I guess there had been some debates between Kariss and Josh earlier that day, which was why he sought out my advice. I proceeded to give Josh the biblical principles, and he took out a napkin to write it all down.

Soon he had a stack of napkins! After some time, Josh took a deep breath and then said, "Whew, I'm good. I'm good." Then he turned to Kariss and said, "Okay, this is how we're going to do it."

What caught my attention when he said that was what Kariss did next. Knowing they had experienced some disagreements on finances earlier, I now saw Kariss place her head on his shoulder and say, "And I'm good too."

I looked at Josh, smiled, and said, "Now that's what I'm talking about!" There is a feeling of well-being that wells up inside of you when you are in alignment with God's will. It's the soul that is brought into the prosperity of peace and understanding. The blessing of the covenant means God even makes those around you to rest as well.

God starts it off with the man. He commands the man to fear Him and take Him seriously. Then the effects of that obedience ripple out to his family, friends, church, community, and world. When we align our hearts under Him in a humble reverence for Him, He will guide us. He will prosper our souls. And then, as the last part of Psalm 25:13 says, our descendants will inherit the land.

A Kingdom Man's Legacy

The third thing you can come to expect from God is legacy. I was seeing that firsthand with Josh and Kariss in that moment of time. It made my heart proud. Legacy is about much more than leaving a name. It's about leaving a lineage of peace, strength, and spiritual impact. We'll look more at the legacy of transferring biblical manhood in the last part of this book, but I wanted to mention it here as well. The treasures of the covenant don't just belong to you. When you apply and use the key to spiritual success, you are also setting up your descendants for their own spiritual achievements.

That's the beauty of this thing called the covenant. God wants to bless you with guidance. He wants to prosper your soul. And He wants to use you to leave a legacy. All He's waiting on in order to do those three things is for you to align your life under Him. When you begin to take Him and His Word seriously on a consistent basis, He will take you to your promised land.

Now, you may have made mistakes along the way. I get that. I understand. You may have lost time. But if you will humble yourself beneath God right now, He can make it so that you do not waste the rest of your life.

I want to challenge you to grab your key to success. It has your name on it. But it can only be used if you submit to God's rule and authority over your life, allowing Him to call the shots. Let Him demonstrate to you that He knows what He is doing. Because He does. Yes, that might require some humility. But the man whom the Bible calls the most humble man on earth, Moses, accomplished an awful lot (see Numbers 12:3). You can too.

My son Jonathan used to breed pit bulls when he was in college. Jonathan is the ultimate entrepreneur and, at that stage in his life, this was one of his businesses. One weekend Jonathan came home with two of his pit bulls. Now, you know I wasn't about to let them into my house. So Jonathan had to leash them to one of our lampposts out back.

A problem occurred when Jonathan went to take the pit bulls for a walk. As he went out to get them, he discovered that they had gotten tangled up around the pole. In order to set them free, he had to pull each of them backward around the pole to unwind the chains. They had to back up before they could move forward. As you might imagine, the pit bulls didn't like being maneuvered in such a way. Pit bulls have really big heads, after all. And big heads don't often like to be told much of anything. The same can be said for a lot of us as men.

Men, you may assume you have enough brains to figure out this thing called life. You might be insisting on going forward according to your own plans for success. But like the pit bulls, the more you push ahead in your own plans, the more you wind up jerked back by the chains. These could be emotional, spiritual, physical, vocational, or relational chains. Whatever kind they are, all chains do one thing: keep you stuck.

I want to encourage you to let God do His work. Let Him lead you, even if it looks like you might be going backward for some time. There are seasons in life when we need to address and untangle the messes we find ourselves in before we can develop and mature enough to handle the successes up ahead. God has a plan for you. He has a destiny for you. But the road to that destiny requires development and discipleship first. As a reminder, a kingdom disciple can be defined as a *believer who takes part in the spiritual-developmental process of progressively learning to live all of life under the lordship of Jesus Christ.*[6] This process of growth from spiritual infancy to spiritual maturity enables the believer to become increasingly more like Christ. Kingdom discipleship is designed to be replicated until Jesus has many in His family who act and think like Him (see Matthew 28:18–20; 2 Timothy 1:13; 2:2; Romans 8:29; 2 Corinthians 3:17–18).

Every Christian man is expected to pursue becoming a full-time, publicly committed follower of Jesus Christ and influencing others to do the same. This involves the daily surrendering of our lives to the authority of Jesus Christ (Luke 9:23). It means accepting the awesome responsibility of regularly transferring our faith and kingdom principles to our families (see Joshua 24:15). This is done as we use mealtime not just for eating but for teaching, praying, blessing, and correcting our offspring (see Psalm 128:3). It also includes leading our family in corporate church worship and service as an active part of God's covenant community of believers.

This also means that every serious Christian man should have relationships with other men who hold one another accountable and responsible for faithfully fulfilling their biblical role and growing in their faith (Galatians 2:11–20). Finally, a Christian man who seriously seeks to be a kingdom disciple seeks to influence the well-being of his community for God and for good as he wisely brings kingdom values into the public square (see Ezekiel 22:30).

For God to unleash His power both in and through you, you have to get rid of the things that prevent you from living as a kingdom disciple. You have to get rid of the big head. You must humble yourself in order to take seriously the Ruler and King. After all, it's His world. He makes up the rules. If you want to make up the rules, then go make your own world. But until then, you need to abide by the rules of the one in charge.

In the next section, "Unleashing Biblical Manhood," we'll explore some of the things that can keep a man stuck—things like emotional strongholds, a lack of confidence, traumatic life experiences, real limitations, and more. Part of living as a kingdom man involves facing and fighting the demons inside so that you can expel them in order to truly rise high. It also involves learning how to apply empathy and strategic connectivity to our relationships in the body of Christ so that we can rise up as kingdom men collectively empowered by God's strength to influence the world around us.

PART TWO

UNLEASHING BIBLICAL MANHOOD

FIVE

GET UP

It's hard to man up if you can't even stand up.

And it seems that we live in a culture of men who can't even stand up right now. They may not be physically lame, but that's not the only kind of lameness. There's mental lameness, when the man does not have the cognitive and emotional capacity to take on his manly responsibilities. There's also social lameness. This is when men expect the government to do for them what God has called them to do in providing for themselves and their families. There exists a plethora of spiritual lameness as well, when men no longer lead devotions, pray with their families, or seek out spiritual answers but instead sit, soak, and sour in front of sports or video games in their flex time.

Lameness comes in all shapes and sizes, no doubt, but it all bears the same characteristic, regardless of how it manifests in a man's life. That characteristic mark of lameness in manhood involves someone else having to do for you what you choose not to do for yourself. It's a failure to exhibit personal responsibility for your thoughts, choices, words, and actions. The blame game goes hand in hand with lameness. As does dominance. After all, if you don't want to take responsibility for your own needs, pressuring someone else to do it for you can seem much easier.

One of the greatest challenges I've discovered over this past decade since *Kingdom Man* came out is the sheer difficulty in calling men to unleash their biblical manhood. It seems that simply taking responsibility for your thoughts and actions has become a lost art. It seems that we might be facing a worldwide plague of personal irresponsibility and entitlement right now. And that just doesn't cut it in the long run.

Imagine if a football coach drafted a star running back with all the potential in the world. He had speed. Moves. Balance. Intuition to read the opposition. All of that and more. On paper, he was already the GOAT (greatest of all time). But when he showed up to practice, he just sat down on the sidelines.

If the coach approached him to get on the field to practice, he'd shrug it off and say he didn't feel like it. Or that he was busy. Or any other excuse that came to mind. Then, on game day, when he failed to make the plays or score the points and the coach asked him why he didn't accomplish the goals of the game, he blamed the opposition. Or, worse yet, he blamed his teammates.

This player wouldn't last long on this team, regardless of his stats, strength, and size when they drafted him. Unleashing a powerful running back requires more than stats and natural ability. It requires intentionality, practice, and responsibility.

Unleashing biblical manhood requires no less.

To unleash the full potential of who you are as a kingdom man, you'll need to first make sure you're up for the challenge. Literally. Manning up starts by getting up. If and when you do not take the divinely ordained responsibility that God has given to you, and every man, by virtue of His created purpose when He made you, then you are lame. Even with fineries decorating your home, office, or social media sites—an irresponsible man is no kingdom man at all.

A Cup or a Hand

In Acts 3, we're told a story about a lame man from whom we can learn. A description of the man is given to us in the first two verses:

> Now Peter and John were going up to the temple at the ninth hour, the hour of prayer. And a man who had been lame from his mother's womb

was being carried along, whom they used to set down every day at the gate of the temple which is called Beautiful, in order to beg alms of those who were entering the temple.

A quick jump over to the next chapter, and we learn that this man was over forty years old (Acts 4:22). So for half of a lifetime, this man had not been able to stand up on his own. He was lame from his mother's womb.

Now, we don't know all of his sociological conditions, although we are given a hint. We don't know if his daddy was in the picture or not, because only his mom is mentioned. But we do know he had to be poor because he was a beggar. We also know that this man's entire life depended upon what other people did for him because we just read that he had been "carried along" to the gate in order to beg. He couldn't even get there on his own. You know you're lame when everyone else has to take care of you like that! This man lived day to day, hand to mouth on trinkets people would toss into a can.

Enter two men who are about to change all of that. Peter and John are headed to the temple at the ninth hour, the hour of prayer. They are taking their lunch hour, presumably, to head over to the temple to connect with the living and true God. A habit every potential kingdom man should pursue, a regular daily time to meet with God. On their way in, they pass the lame man and our story unfolds.

"Can you spare a dime?" he may have said.

"Can you help a brother out? Give me a little something, would you?" he might have said as he held out his can. "I just need to make it another day. Come on, man!" But the words stopped Peter in his tracks this day, unlike the other days when the same song had been sung. Peter just wasn't going to stand for it anymore. He knew this man had the capacity for so much more than begging. So he stared right at him and said, "Look at us!" (v. 4).

Now, if Peter had to tell him to "look at us," that means he wasn't looking at them to begin with. If he had to be told to pay attention to them, that gives us great insight into this lame man. He had gotten so used to begging that he wasn't even looking at the people he was asking for money from. Head down. Eyes down. Hand out. Shake the can, most likely with a heart of shame. Life had beaten this man down for so long that all he could do was hold his head down and hope for a scrap of kindness.

People pass by and he mumbles his words—words he probably even says while he's dreaming, because he's said them so often and for so long. "Please, sir. Please, ma'am. Can you spare something?"

Peter knew he needed this man's undivided attention. He needed him to focus. He needed him to hear him, in his heart. If this man truly wanted a solution to unleash his abilities and manhood, he'd need to pay close attention to Peter right then. Healing and empowerment are not a one-way gift through the touch of a magic wand. To be unleashed in your fullest potential requires your desire, responsibility, and focus. That's why Jesus would often ask the question "Do you want to be made well?" He didn't just walk around tapping people on the head, bestowing health and healing on whomever was near. Rather, Jesus would ask if the person was willing to be made whole. He did this because, if he or she was not willing, He couldn't help them. Wholeness and strength have to come from within. You don't light a candle by putting a flame to the outer wax. You have to light the wick.

You also don't place a candle under direct sunlight, not if you don't want to waste it. But far too many men are content with being like the flicker of a candle under the noonday sun. Unnoticed. Leaving no impact. Making no mark on a world that desperately needs kingdom men. A person can get so used to being a failure, or so used to being defeated, that he begins to think it is impossible that his life could be better. Lameness can, and often does, set in as an addiction. I know we rarely hear of lameness when we speak about addictions, but it's a big one. It's when a man gets used to not manning up, not standing up, and not becoming what God designed him to be.

Peter needed to see if this man truly wanted to be whole again. He asked for his undivided attention. We read in verse 5 that he got it, with a caveat of caution, of course. It says, "And he began to give them his attention, expecting to receive something from them." He looked at them. He paid attention. But he didn't expect much. Maybe just a little more than a trinket. The lame man looked, but that doesn't mean he listened. Most likely his eyes went to their hands and not their faces.

It's like that feeling you get when you receive a birthday card in the mail. You open it without much anticipation of what's written inside. You skim those soft-sounding words wishing you well, but your real intention is to open that card and shake it! In fact, as you slide it out of the envelope, you do a little movement so it faces down, just in case something needs to drop out. You know what I'm talking about—we've all done it. I know I do it too. And if nothing does come out, sometimes I'll even shake it twice.

The lame man looked at Peter and John, probably with a bit of hope. Hope for enough for two meals, or even three. His eyes shifted between their hands, their pockets, and their faces. He was paying attention now, only to hear what undoubtedly hit him hard when Peter said, "I do not possess silver and gold" (v. 6).

If it were me, I would have probably responded with "You have got to be kidding me!" Or maybe something that sounded more spiritual, like "Excuse me?"

Peter had told him to look at him. He'd told him to pay attention. And now he's telling him that he's got nothing to give. The bank is broke. The man was asking him for money, but Peter just told him he didn't have any of that. A look of confusion was most likely all he could muster in return. He probably looked away.

What the lame man failed to realize was that money is not the endgame. See, most men think money truly is. They think that happiness equates to how much money you've got at your disposal. But happiness has nothing to do with money. Money isn't about to solve your problems. In fact, as I've spent decades counseling men, I've come to discover how oftentimes the problems escalate as money increases—not the other way around.

Far too many men believe that if they can make more money, get a better job, take on a second job, or do whatever will get their investments to grow, they'll be happy. They'll be satisfied. They'll feel peace. But that's a very wrong assumption. There are many things money can't buy. Money can't buy health. It can't buy relational harmony. It can't buy respect, honor, character, or esteem. When things go south in any of those areas and others, and money is all you've got working for you, you'll find out the real value of money. You'll quickly learn that money isn't all it's cracked up to be. There's so much more that really matters.

But it's very easy to forget that. I understand. That's why we need reminders like this biblical account to help us stay focused on the root of our solutions. This man was like so many men; he'd gotten focused on the wrong thing. He was praying for the wrong thing, like many do today. Praying for a better job, bigger house, more clout, notoriety, social media followers, or video views. Men are praying for stuff when God wants to give more than stuff. He wants to give significance, strength, stability, and identity.

All the stuff in the world doesn't mean a hill of beans if you are so broken, empty, or alone that you cannot enjoy it and you don't have anyone with whom to enjoy it. Stuff never made a man smile the way that satisfaction, purpose, and even service does. Yet, even so, we've got a world focused on stuff. And don't get me wrong, stuff is okay—as long as the stuff is kept in check with God's rightful rule in a person's life. All this lame man wanted was enough to keep his lameness intact. God is not concerned with keeping our lameness intact. He's concerned with changing our lameness so we are not lame anymore.

Peter told the man that he didn't have *stuff* for him. He didn't have silver or gold to give. But he did have something even more valuable than that. He had something better.

"What I do have," Peter said with a commanding voice, "I give to you: In the name of Jesus Christ the Nazarene—walk!" (v. 6). In other words, he told him that in the name of Jesus Christ the Nazarene, he was to stop being lame. He told him to get up. Stand up. Stop asking for a tip. Stop rattling his tin can. Stop looking for leftovers.

Get up.

Man up.

Be responsible.

What's more, he was to do all of this through the power of a Name. In the Bible, names matter. Names have meanings. Names are never mere nomenclature. People weren't named because it sounded nice, or their parents were copying a celebrity somewhere, or their mom suggested it—*strongly*. Names carried weight and character and were often tied to the future. That's why, throughout Scripture, when God was about to do something new in a place or with a person, He would often change the name.

Abram became Abraham.

Jacob became Israel.

Simon became Peter.

Saul became Paul.

All through the Bible, God is switching around names because He's switching up identities or purposes tied to His kingdom roles. A person was given a new name designed to fit the reputation or character of his or her new path. Names held power tied to purpose.

The name of Jesus, of course, held—and holds—the power above all power. That's why we read later in this biblical account that people were literally asking Peter and John in whose name they had done this miracle. We read this in Acts 4:7: "When they had placed them in the center, they began to inquire, 'By what power, or in what name, have you done this?'" The leaders wanted to know under whose authority this lame man now walked.

Peter didn't hesitate in his answer, but he threw a descriptive phrase in that he also used when he first healed the man and that is worth looking at further. But first, he said, "Let it be known to all of you and to all the people of Israel, that by the name of Jesus Christ the Nazarene, whom you crucified, whom God raised from the dead—by this name this man stands here before you in good health" (Acts 4:10).

The descriptive phrase Peter threw in wasn't "the Lord." Nor was it "our Savior." Peter didn't say, "Jesus Christ, the King." No, he used a descriptive phrase that could lead to a bit of head scratching, actually. Rather than appealing to the powerful might of Jesus Christ through titles like Messiah, Risen Lord, or Ruler, Peter referred to Jesus Christ as the *Nazarene*. He said:

"In the name of Jesus Christ the Nazarene" (Acts 3:6).

"By the name of Jesus Christ the Nazarene" (Acts 4:10).

Peter wanted to make sure everyone knew whose power had done this feat: It was Jesus the Nazarene. Yet why draw attention to something so seemingly unimportant as Nazareth? Jesus wasn't even born in Nazareth. He was born in Bethlehem. Sure, He was raised in Nazareth, but what was this small town of Nazareth to anyone anyhow?

We garner the overall feel toward this town by looking at Nathanael's flippant remark when Philip tried to get him to go see Jesus for the first time. As recorded for us in John 1:46, Nathanael (who would later go on to be one of Jesus' twelve disciples) responded to Philip's nudging with this: "Can any good thing come out of Nazareth?"

Can any good thing come out of Nazareth? It's phrased more like a statement, or a rhetorical question at best. And it's a pretty revealing statement at that. Nazareth was a no-name town. The kind of town that might not even have a stoplight. The kind of town of which you might be told, "Don't blink when you go through, because you could miss it." It was a hood town, as we say where I come from. It held no prestige. It had produced no one of prominence. The local school gym was probably named School Gym, rather than after someone of power or influence who had once lived there.

All Nazareth had was a bunch of poor people, most likely racked by real-world problems, high crime, low education, and no hope. Nathanael's question came loaded with hints of a town plagued by systemic issues that ran centuries deep. Everyone knew nothing good ever came out of Nazareth—it just wasn't able to provide a good start.

Why is this important to know? It's important because a lot of us are from Nazareth. You might be from Nazareth. I know I am. I grew up in urban Baltimore in row houses, most of which are littered with drugs today. The majority of my male classmates are either dead or in jail. Maybe you don't hail from urban Baltimore, but there are other Nazareths out there.

Perhaps you didn't have a good beginning upon which to build. Maybe your parents fought or divorced early on. Maybe you didn't come from a nice neighborhood or a school system whose funding indicated that they took your future seriously. Maybe you had to raise yourself because your mom worked three jobs. Or maybe you lived in the suburbs, but you were abused, neglected, or pacified with stuff. You were kept busy to keep you away from any real relationship at home. Whatever the case, Nazareth is where many of us started.

That's why it's so critical to know that Jesus was from Nazareth too. Since Jesus came from this no-name place, He can meet any man in any place at any time, even when your life seems lame. He can turn it around and set you on your feet, if you will just look to the Jesus from Nazareth. The Jesus from the hood. The Jesus from no hope, no opportunity, and no way out—let alone up.

The truth of this reality strips us of any excuses we might have claimed, like "If it weren't for him," or "If it weren't for them," or "If it weren't for that circumstance, or my background, or my limitations." All that is real. I get it. I'm not saying it's not real. What I am saying is that in the name of Jesus Christ, the one from *Nazareth*, you don't need to be whining anymore. You can get up. You can walk. You can be responsible. You are no longer to see yourself as a victim. Your relationship with Jesus Christ makes you an overcomer (1 John 5:1–4).

> Your relationship with Jesus Christ makes you an overcomer.

It's time to own your life. It's time to take charge of who you are. Stop letting other people's thoughts, words, or actions drive you down. There is power in the name of Jesus, even when there's no money on the table. Because in His name, you can get up and unleash your full potential.

Grab a Hand

That's exactly what the lame man did when Peter reached down, seized him by the hand, and pulled him up. The lame man stood. But another problem we face today is that we have too few Peters willing to grab a hand and lift someone up. Peter didn't just pronounce the power of God upon this man. He didn't stand there with arms folded, head held high, and give him a nod. No, Peter knew this man needed a jolt. He needed a push. He needed someone to both encourage him and help him stand on his own. So, as we see in Acts 3:7, "seizing him by the right hand, he raised him up; and immediately his feet and his ankles were strengthened."

We've got a generation of men around us who need someone to raise them up to stand. The problem is that the wrong group of men have been grabbing them and taking them in the wrong direction. We need godly kingdom men to lead them toward health, wholeness, responsibility, and biblical manhood. Peter didn't just pray. He didn't hold a webinar for a fee. He didn't speak at a conference, write a book, write a blog post, or create a podcast. Scripture tells us clearly that Peter seized the man by his right hand and raised him up. What's more, the man let him. See, it takes both sides working together for discipleship to take place.

Have you ever picked up one of your sleepy kids, nieces or nephews, or grandkids who just don't want to put forth any of their own effort? A forty-five-pound kid can feel like they weigh a hundred pounds because they are just limp, letting you do all of the work. And when you go to set them down, if they are very tired, their legs just crumple beneath them, so you have to lift them back up again. That's a big difference from picking up the kid who is running to you and using his or her strength to hold themselves up as well. It almost feels like nothing. Because when both work together, things feel lighter.

Peter reached down to grab the man's hand. The man allowed himself to be grab-able. The result? An immediate strengthening of his feet and ankles. He now stood on his own. This is following forty years of no use of his legs at all. He'd been crippled from his mother's womb. His legs had undoubtedly atrophied. Not only was he crippled but he was also weak after forty years, because strength comes through use.

But when the power of Jesus' name set in, we see that he was immediately healed and strengthened. There were no twelve-step programs or twelve-miles-of-rehab programs. It didn't take years or decades of counseling to get this man healed. God overcame a lifetime of lameness in a moment.

It happened suddenly.

Suddenly. It's a word you'll hear me repeat due to its importance. Because one thing you need to understand as we dive deeper into this concept of unleashing biblical manhood is that God doesn't need time. He can do whatever He wants whenever He wants to, on a dime. He's just waiting for you to look at Him in order to receive a supernatural infusion of His power. The moment you are ready, God is too. When God wants to move, He can move faster than an X-15 fighter tearing across the sky at Mach 6. This lame man's healing happened in an instant. Then he jumped up, stood tall, and began to walk (v. 8).

> God is just waiting for you to look at Him in order to receive a supernatural infusion of His power.

Healing That Makes an Impact

He didn't crawl. He didn't limp. He didn't sit back down. No, the man walked. And the passage tells us that he walked right into the temple himself—leaping and praising God.

Let me tell you what will ignite your prayer and praise life like nothing else: when God intervenes. When God gives you a testimony, you don't need a program, Bible study, or worship song to prompt you to praise Him. This formerly lame man jumped right up and headed straight into the temple to get his praise on! Because when God moves in your life, you don't worry about how you look anymore. You don't concern yourself with whether your praise is cute anymore. You don't need to be seditty or sophisticated and use words like *thee* and *thou*. No, when God moves in your life you leap. Jump. Run. Praise. Worship. Tell others. Enjoy. Honor. And dance.

That's what unleashing biblical manhood looks like. What's more, it leaves an impact. How do I know? We read in Acts 4:4 the result of this man's life and testimony. It says, "But many of those who had heard the message believed; and the number of the men came to be about five thousand."

What started with one man quickly turned into five thousand men believing and being unleashed into an opportunity for a full expression of biblical manhood. That's because when God gives you a testimony, He enables you to touch others with it too.

God wants you whole and strong not just for you. He wants the others in your circle of influence to stand up too. If all you are doing is participating in church or attending a small group or throwing God a prayer here or there, you are not demonstrating to others who God has created you to be.

If and when God transforms any aspect of your life (emotions, addictions, relationships, and more), you've got to make it known. You've got to share this truth with others. Don't be ashamed. Don't be shy. God has given you your testimony for a reason. Don't miss the purpose of the miracle, which is to draw others toward their miracles.

The good news of the lame man is that it's not too late. His life was halfway over, but he got a new start. Similarly, God can meet you where you are, even if you feel like your life is nearly over. He can reach down, lift you up, and turn you loose—for His glory and others' good.

It doesn't matter if you're from Nazareth either. Your background doesn't define you. What you do right now, this very moment, reveals who you are.

I love the movie *Rocky V*. What man doesn't? By *Rocky V*, the prize-fighter has grown older and has retired. He's lost a step or two along the way. His moves are slower. His eyes are not as sharp. But his heart is still strong. So Rocky seeks to invest all of his training and insight into a young up-and-comer named Tommy Gunn. Rocky works with Tommy long enough for Tommy to climb the ladder and become the heavyweight champion of the world himself.

The problem is that all of Tommy's success, which is due to Rocky's training, goes to his head. He has money. He has fame. He has power. He also has pride. During the last scene, Tommy winds up knocking Rocky's brother-in-law to the ground with a sucker punch during an argument at a bar. After the punch, Tommy then insults the one who has trained him and given him all he now enjoys. Yes, he turns his rage toward Rocky. What's worse, he does so by insulting Rocky's own son.

All of that proves too much for Rocky, so he tells him to take it outside. What started as a quarrel quickly erupts into a street fight.

The problem for Rocky, though, is that Tommy is young. He is fast, strong, and angry. It isn't long before Rocky is facedown in the gutter, beaten down. Yet while he lies there, you can guess what happens: The music in the movie begins to build. You know the tune. And as it does, memories of past training and past victories flood into Rocky's mind. He reflects on beating Apollo Creed, Clubber Lang, and Ivan Drago. He sees his many wins and the times he has overcome. All of those memories contribute to the strength brewing inside.

But then, Rocky remembers something even more powerful than his past victories. He remembers his trainer, Mickey. Mickey, a short man with great might, had stood over him when he had gotten knocked down. Rocky can hear his words clearly: "Get up! Get up! Get up, you bum! Mickey loves you!"[1]

The music rises in a crescendo. Rocky lifts his head. He shakes off the punch. Then he stares at Tommy Gunn walking away in the distance and he yells, "Yo, Tommy! . . . One more round!"[2]

Rocky found strength and power he didn't previously possess because he remembered someone who believed in him and who reminded him of what he could do.

Men, I don't care how long you've been down in the gutters of life. I don't care how long you may have felt defeated as a man. Jesus Christ is standing over you today and yelling to you right now: "Get up! Get up! Get up, you kingdom man! Jesus loves you!"

It's time to pull yourself up and take charge of that which seeks to defeat you. It's time to go one more round.

GET OVER

It's time to get a bit more personal, as many of you might relate to what I'm about to say. I've chosen to share this real-life illustration with you because I want you to get a greater glimpse into the importance of getting over the things that can hold us back. Overcoming obstacles can be difficult, especially if we don't easily identify these obstacles right off the bat.

When I mention the need to overcome a stronghold or break an addictive behavior, what comes to your mind? Unfortunately, for most men, the things that instantly come to mind are drugs and pornography. For whatever reason, our culture considers these the major strongholds in life. Things like drug addiction, pornography, or living like a rolling stone are damaging strongholds and destructive cycles, but they aren't the only things that can keep a man bound.

However, our laser focus on these so-called "major" addictions can create a barrier to overcoming our own seemingly-not-so-major issues. I say that it can become a barrier because we might wind up looking at other people's struggles (if we don't have a problem with drugs or pornography) and shrug off our own. *At least I don't do what that guy does,* we think, as we proceed to pat ourselves on the back. All the while our own great purposes, destinies, and legacies are being swallowed whole by Satan through our own strongholds we refuse to identify.

It can get even worse, though, when we give in to thinking prideful thoughts of not being bound by the major struggles, even though we are bound just as firmly by more subtle ones. So now we not only have our subtle strongholds, but we've also got pride to overcome! Men, Satan doesn't care if your stronghold is considered *major* by cultural standards or not. He just wants you bound.

So I want to share one of my past struggles with you in an effort to speak openly about a stronghold that many men probably face, but few even consider to be a stronghold at all. It's time we reexamined and identified common strongholds for men that go beyond the big two or three. We need to be more honest about the variety of things that are holding us back—even things like laziness, irresponsibility, anxiety, and people-pleasing are strongholds and addictive behaviors that break a man's ability to leave a kingdom mark.

So the one I want to share with you that I fell into at some point is the stronghold of work. The reason we are not always aware of this as a stronghold is because we recognize its results in a very positive way. Success is applauded. Achievement brings glory. Busy has become the new badge of honor these days. With all of that to contend with, and more, it's easy to become addicted to the stronghold of work.

Anyone who knows me well would probably call me a workaholic. I love to work. If I'm not working, I'm usually reading books on the Bible, theology, and philosophy, underlining important points, and recording my personal notes. I have thousands upon thousands of notes—handwritten the old-fashioned way on yellow pads, or at times I write them inside my books. If you walk into my office, you will probably see a stack of a hundred sheets of notes just sitting out—most likely because I've been looking at them while preparing a sermon or something I'm writing.

I spent the previous decade going through the entire Bible—studying, examining, and writing notes on each book to compile into the Bible commentary and the study Bible I released not long ago. I'd find myself getting up at three or four in the morning on a regular basis to have this quiet time to study, reflect, and write. This work came on top of an already very full work week for me as a senior pastor of a 10,000-plus member church with more than 350 acres of property to manage, over 100 various

ministries, and a staff of more than 300. In addition, I'm president of a
national broadcast ministry and a frequent guest speaker—and I write a
lot of books. I love to work. Just about as much as I love being a man. If
you've read *Kingdom Man*, then you know what I mean by that!

But for the purposes of this chapter and our focus on unleashing your
biblical manhood, I want to emphasize how too much of a good thing can
actually work against you. For starters, work, in and of itself, is a good
thing. It brings good to those who are impacted by it, and it gives those
who enjoy it a deep sense of satisfaction. In fact, Scripture commends
work as a gift. We read,

> There is nothing better for a man than to eat and drink and tell himself
> that his labor is good. This also I have seen that it is from the hand of God.
>
> Ecclesiastes 2:24

> Furthermore, as for every man to whom God has given riches and wealth,
> He has also empowered him to eat from them and to receive his reward
> and rejoice in his labor; this is the gift of God.
>
> Ecclesiastes 5:19

> Let the favor of the Lord our God be upon us; and confirm for us the work
> of our hands; yes, confirm the work of our hands.
>
> Psalm 90:17

> Whatever you do, do your work heartily, as for the Lord rather than for men.
>
> Colossians 3:23

Work is good. It's a gift from God. But keep in mind, a lot of things start
out as good and wind up as a stronghold. Sex, in the context of marriage,
is good. Pornography is a sin and stronghold. Eating a delicious meal is
good. Gluttony that debilitates your health is a stronghold. Exercise is
good. Obsession about your physical looks and personal pride are strongholds. Satan often starts with something good and seeks to twist it into
a stronghold in order to hook us into a spirit of addiction that keeps us
bound.

Which brings me to my confession. Many years back, I began to notice a pattern creeping up with regard to my work and my vacation schedule. One of my wife's greatest gifts to me and to our family over our forty-nine years of marriage was her emphasis on family time and rest. I know that I have accomplished as much as I have because I avoided burnout due to her loving intervention time and again. One of the family routines she established for our home early on was our summer vacation schedule. Each year we set aside the month of August to unwind, recharge, bond, and spend greater focused time with each other and with the Lord.

But I began to notice a number of years ago that for about five years in a row, whenever August rolled around or I took an extended break for Christmas and New Year's, I got physically sick. The sickness wouldn't always be the same thing, but the pattern of illness in general showed up almost like clockwork. Sometimes I got the flu or had a persistent cough that would last nearly the entire vacation. Another time I developed gout and had to be in a wheelchair in the airport as we made our way back home from our island getaway in Bermuda. Yet another time I got kidney stones and had to be hospitalized on what was to be a peaceful trip to Hawaii. On another occasion I wound up in severe pain for nearly the entire two weeks on a cruise due to a tooth abscess.

Whether severe or mild, something tended to creep up when I took time off from work. Conversely, I was almost never sick while working. In fact, after four decades of preaching on Sundays, I've only missed one Sunday due to sickness. Ever. These two diametrically opposed realities eventually caught my attention and caused me to stop and think. Something was going on, and I needed to get to the bottom of it. I needed to address it in order to overcome its hold on my life. Rest is critical. I knew that. But for some reason, I was not allowing myself to rest.

In the process of examining my thoughts, I came to realize some important things about my view of work and rest. Some of those thoughts were good, and some were not. Eventually I was able to identify these thoughts and correct the ones that were not so good, and almost immediately I saw an improvement in my ability to rest and enjoy the time away that I needed to recharge.

Essentially, I had gotten so caught up in all that was going on at work that I had resigned myself to the concept of rest, but I no longer embraced it. Doing something because you know you're "supposed to" doesn't always have the same positive impact that doing something because you want to strengthen yourself does. God has stated many times in Scripture that work is good. But He has also stated that rest is good. We read,

> By the seventh day God completed His work which He had done, and He rested on the seventh day from all His work which He had done.
>
> Genesis 2:2

> In vain you rise early and stay up late, toiling for food to eat—for he grants sleep to those he loves.
>
> Psalm 127:2 NIV

> Jesus said to them, "The Sabbath was made for man, and not man for the Sabbath."
>
> Mark 2:27

> And He said to them, "Come away by yourselves to a secluded place and rest a while." (For there were many people coming and going, and they did not even have time to eat.)
>
> Mark 6:31

Since that season when I transformed my mind through God's Word on the importance of rest (and God's ability to provide ongoing favor and productivity in the midst of our rest), I've been fairly free of illness during vacations and holiday breaks. This is because I addressed the distorted belief system at the root of the problem and not just the symptom.

Overcoming addictions—whether these are addictions to work, approval, physique, status, drugs, alcohol, or something else—begins with identifying the root of the problem and addressing it in your mind. These issues must be addressed for you to fully unleash your biblical manhood as a kingdom man. If you don't, then addictions will leave their negative impacts on your life through broken relationships, broken bodies, broken dreams, and destroyed lives. Isn't it time to be set free from the symptoms of wrong thinking? It's up to you to get started on the path to wholeness and victorious kingdom living.

You Can Overcome

A POW is a prisoner of war—a person who has been captured by the enemy and is held hostage in the context of a conflict. The opposing forces control the prisoner's living conditions, activities, and movements. Many men live like POWs, but rather than being prisoners of war, they're prisoners of addictive behavior. They have been captured by the enemy, and there appears to be no way of escape. They feel trapped in situations and circumstances that the world labels as addiction. Drugs, sex, pornography, alcohol, relationships, negative self-talk, work, food, gambling, spending—these things can become the go-to coping mechanisms for life's pain, disappointments, and boredom. When an action or activity begins to influence you more than you influence it, it can leave you feeling trapped—as if there is no way out.

I sometimes compare addictive behavior to quicksand. The harder you try to get out of a situation, the deeper you sink. Human methods can never set you free from a spiritual stranglehold on your life. Rather, these attempts will make you sink faster.

Another problem that arises when someone is sinking in quicksand involves focus. As illustrated by Peter's sinking beneath the waves, where you look matters. If a person stares only at the sand surrounding them, they will miss the stick being held out to them that they must grasp to be dragged out.

One of the worst things I have seen men focus on when it comes to the area of spiritual strongholds is how long they've been stuck. I know this because I counsel men on a regular basis, and inevitably it's one of the first things men tell me when they come in.

"Pastor, I've been dealing with this for X number of years," or "I just don't know how to get over something that's held me bound for X years!" For whatever reason, they think the length of time a person's been stuck hinders their exit.

But I'm here to remind you that you are free to get over whatever it is that has gripped you as soon as you decide to do just that. How long you've been bound doesn't matter. You can get up. You can get over the obstacles that keep you down.

Other questions I often hear when I counsel men through the pains and disappointments of life reveal worry over whether it is too late to do anything great with the time they've got left. So many men have asked me over the years, "Is it too late for me? Is it too late for God to do something with me?" Those questions come out of a deep place where they feel they have failed miserably and have forfeited their God-given destiny, most likely due to addictive strongholds. When asked that question, I always have one response: "It is not too late. It is never too late for God."

An important principle to remember when contemplating that question is that God frequently uses broken people to accomplish His kingdom agenda on earth. Time after time in Scripture, we read about the broken people God raised up in a powerful way. He used Moses, a murderer, to deliver the Hebrew slaves. He used Jacob, a liar and a trickster, to fulfill His promise to Abraham. He even used Peter after his denial, Solomon after his idolatry, and Samson after his multiple failures. If God redeemed their lives, He can redeem your life too.

> God frequently uses broken people to accomplish His kingdom agenda on earth.

Brokenness should never keep you bound. Rather, it should release you into a greater life of purpose through what you have learned, because a truly broken person understands the reality of John 15:5, where Jesus says, "Apart from Me you can do nothing." A broken man who has learned both surrender to and dependence on God is a force to be reckoned with.

Yet, it is difficult to even see your future when you are staring at your past, or even the damaging effects of the present. But let me remind you what happens midway through any football game. The teams go to their respective locker rooms at halftime. Halftime is a time for rest and assessment. It is a time to regather and look at how things have been going so far in the game, as well as to decide what adjustments need to be made for the remaining part of the competition.

While the first half of any football game is important, it is not determinative. There have been numerous teams over the years who were ahead at halftime only to lose when the game was done. And there have been numerous teams over the years who were losing at halftime, but by the time the game came to an end, they had turned things around. Until the final whistle is blown, the game is still up for grabs.

The same is true in life. You might be in your first quarter, second quarter, or halftime, but if you are still here, it is not over. Your clock is still ticking. There is plenty of life yet to live. Not only that, but your first half does not have to determine the outcome of the game. Maybe you have made mistakes and poor decisions and have experienced failures, real struggle, and loss. Maybe life has dealt you some harsh blows. But you are still here. It is not too late for God to take you straight to the plan that He has for you. It is not too late for God to lead you into your glorious tomorrow.

God looks at your future, while the enemy tries to keep you in your past. God says, "You can, in spite of what has been done!" The enemy says, "You can't, because of what you have done!" God will never define you by your past issues, but the enemy will try to confine you by them. Whether it is the good, bad, or ugly that dominates your first half, it is Satan's goal to keep you chained there. But my charge to you as we go through this book together is to never let your yesterday keep you from your tomorrow. Learn from yesterday, but don't live in it. Your victory comes through learning and then applying what you've learned. Unleashing biblical manhood starts with your thoughts.

After all, Satan's number one strategy to keep you in unhealthy addictive cycles is to mess with your mind. He likes to plant thoughts in your mind, repeating them over and over until you start to think they are your own thoughts. When Satan told Eve she would be like God if she ate of the fruit, whose thought was that? Was that Eve's thought? No. That thought came straight from Satan himself. In fact, he'd had the same thought before, as we read in Isaiah 14:14: "I will make myself like the Most High." It was Satan's thought, but he planted it in Eve's mind.

Planted Thoughts

If you've seen the movie *Inception*, you've seen this depicted dramatically. The movie is about planting a thought in someone's mind that will change the course of events for generations to come. It's a brilliant movie, and it helps us understand Satan's strategy for derailing each of us from our God-given destinies.

When you tell yourself, *I can't overcome this addiction*, whose thought is that? Or when you think, *I have to have this drink*, whose thought is that? Or when you entertain such thoughts as *I am nothing. I have no value. I don't have power over my emotions of lust or anger*, who is doing the talking? We know these thoughts come from Satan because they are all lies, and he is the father of lies (John 8:44).

Satan has been working his deception game for a very long time. He knows how to cleverly plant his thoughts in your mind and cause you to believe they are true. He did this to King David, as we read in 1 Chronicles 21:1: "Then Satan stood up against Israel and moved David to number Israel." Satan gave David the thought to start counting to see exactly how strong the nation really was. David decided to take a census, thinking this was his own idea. But taking this census was a sin because it demonstrated that David was relying on human strength rather than depending on God, and God judged Israel for David's sin. David was later judged harshly for this sin and had to pay the price for his pride.

We see another example of Satan planting thoughts in someone's mind in John 13:2. He "put into the heart of Judas" the idea to betray Jesus.

In Acts 5:3, we see that Satan used the same approach with Ananias. Peter asks Ananias, "Why has Satan filled your heart to lie to the Holy Spirit?" In this case, Satan had given Ananias and his wife, Sapphira, the idea of selling a piece of property, giving some of the money to the church, and pretending that they had given the full amount. This thought cost both of them much more than money. It cost them their lives.

Satan makes quick work of planting and directing thoughts. But his thoughts do not have to have the last word. You have the power to control your own thoughts. How should you respond to Satan's thoughts? The same way Jesus did when Peter tried to keep Him from going to the cross. Peter told Jesus, "God forbid it, Lord! This shall never happen to You."

To which Jesus replied, "Get behind Me, Satan!" (Matthew 16:22–23). The words came from Peter, but the thoughts came from Satan. When Satan gets into your mind, he gets into your actions. The key to overcoming addictive behavior is to take your thoughts captive.

Scripture tells us that as a man *thinks*, so that man *is* (Proverbs 23:7). This passage is the foundation for overcoming all addictive behavior. Memorize that verse. Understand its impact on all you do.

Men, your addiction doesn't stem from the item or vice itself. It stems from your thoughts. Your addiction is rooted, and fed, in your mind. Once Satan plants thoughts in your mind and you allow them to continue—even helping them to grow through your actions or inaction—those thoughts then transfer biologically and physiologically to your emotions.

Stick with me as we explore some quick science, because it's important for you to understand what is going on inside of you. Your *limbic system* is the biological system that translates these thoughts into what are called *ligands*. Based on the specific thought, these ligands trigger a chain reaction of emotions similar to what you've experienced in the past.

Ligands are made up of *peptides, hormones*, and other bodily communicators. Once these ligands are released, they travel through your body toward their target receptors. This process happens almost instantaneously, which is why you can have a nearly automatic emotional response to a thought. Once the ligands reach their receptors, a vibration is made between the two of them, allowing the cells in that part of your body to open their walls and receive the message. This changes the cell itself, causing it to make new proteins, divide, or do any number of things, depending on the particular cells.

The process of thoughts triggering emotions that then impact your cells is so powerful that it causes physiological changes, such as psychosomatic illnesses or even healings when you're given a placebo you believe in (a nonmedicated substitute). It also affects your mood and actions as your body responds to the emotion.

Have you ever noticed how your entire body reacts when a car swerves toward you? Or when you sense something dangerous approaching you?

Have you noticed how your body naturally relaxes when the danger is avoided? These are just simple examples of your body's response to emotions.

Satan seeks to capture your thoughts because they are what will trigger your emotions, which in turn influence your actions. Thus, addictions are prolonged through emotional manipulations. The alcoholism, drug abuse, endless spending, excessive working, pornography viewing, ongoing masturbation, or obsession with power is a reaction to an emotion that has affected your body's cravings and needs. Understanding the physiological impact of your thoughts on your emotions, and ultimately on your body, helps to underscore where the battle for your freedom exists. It is entirely in your thoughts.

Gain mastery of your thoughts and you will master your emotions. Master your emotions and you will overcome any addiction or stronghold that enslaves you.

That's why we can't expect someone to make lasting changes just because we tell them to calm down or to stop drinking, misusing women, swearing, binge-watching, or doing whatever they are doing. We can't talk someone out of an addiction simply by explaining the negative effects of what they are doing to themselves and those around them. We need to address their thoughts and get to the root of the lies that are causing the emotions that lead them to mask their pain through addiction. The same holds true for you—you need to address your thoughts and uncover the lies that must be uprooted and replaced with truth in order to stop any negative or addictive behaviors.

The Power of the Word

Not too long ago I had the privilege of sitting down with Everett Brown and getting to know him on a more personal level. I had met Everett and heard his story when he accompanied his brother, NFL host James Brown, to speaking events or other engagements. I had heard how God had done a miraculous work in Everett's life by releasing him from serious drug addictions. But it was only when I got to sit down and talk with Everett that I heard his emphasis on the power of God's Word to overcome strongholds.

Now, I know the power of God's Word. I believe in it. I'm a preacher. If I don't believe in the power of God's Word, I should get a different job. God's Word changes lives. It's the active sword of God himself. But when I sat down with Everett Brown to talk about how God had set him free from decades of drug addiction, I was reminded of the sheer strength of the Word of God. His story encouraged me greatly, so I wanted to share it with you.

Everett struggled for over half his life with four major addictions: crack cocaine, pornography, womanizing, and seeking approval. Despite his best efforts, he never found a way to get over the hold these four demons had on his life. Everett shared with me how he went in and out of multiple rehab centers. No expense was spared. He tried it all. But regardless of what they taught him, he wound up right back in his self-defeating, negative, addictive patterns as soon as he got out.

That is, until he tried an addiction recovery center he had heard me recommend in a sermon. It's called America's Keswick, and in their variety of programs, they have one for overcoming addiction that focuses only on the Word of God. The time in the center allows a person to experience the full effects of a transformed mind by continually thinking on the truths of Scripture. One of the rules is that the person in recovery can only use God's Word. They can't bring in other books, music, or anything.

"I want to bring Tony Evans's app in to listen to sermons," Everett said he had told them when he was entering his ninth stint in rehab. "And some of his books," Everett continued. But they didn't let him. It was God's Word and nothing else.

Everett put it like this: "We got three square meals a day. A little bit of work on the grounds to stay active. No TV. No books. Just God's Word." And by the end of his time in rehab, Everett said he was set free for the very first time in his life. Memorizing God's transformative Word had worked. This was several years ago, and since then he's enjoyed a satisfying marriage, ministry to others, and the peace of the Lord through a life no longer broken and bound. Our conversation continued as Everett shared about what God was doing in his life. And what impacted me most was that after listing off a litany of health challenges he now faces due to over fifty years of damaging decisions and addictions, he smiled with one of the most authentic smiles I'd ever seen and said, "But I'm free!" The smile was contagious.

"All these problems and you are free at the same time?" I asked, just wanting to hear it again.

"Tony, I'm free," Everett said, almost as if that one phrase alone summarized the very significance of life itself.

Freedom is valuable. Freedom from Satan's manipulations, distortions, and destructive influences opens the gateway to experiencing your own personal greatness as a kingdom man. But freedom is never free. It always comes at a cost.

Tear Down the Fortress

One such cost is effort. Freedom can be defined as *the release from illegitimate bondage so that you can choose to exercise responsibility in maximizing all that you were created to be.*[2] The freedom actualized through a kingdom perspective in facing obstacles and challenges and in embracing God's sovereignty generates a faith more powerful than any human weapon or system of philosophy ever could. It accesses God's grace in such a way as to grant a freedom that is not dependent upon externals. This is the only true, authentic freedom, as it manifests God's ability to bring about good in any and every situation surrendered to Him (see Galatians 5:1–4; John 8:32–36; 2 Corinthians 3:17).

This freedom only comes through willingness to do battle in the spiritual realm. You must war with the enemy at the source of the bondage itself, in your mind. Satan doesn't just stick a tiny thought in you hoping that it will stay put. No, Scripture tells us plainly that the devil erects fortresses of false thoughts. Paul tells us this in no uncertain terms:

> For though we walk in the flesh, we do not war according to the flesh, for the weapons of our warfare are not of the flesh, but divinely powerful for the destruction of fortresses.
>
> 2 Corinthians 10:3–4

When medieval fortresses were built, they were nearly impregnable. If you have toured one or seen them in movies, you know that their massive walls provided intimidating defenses against enemy soldiers. Scaling the wall to bring the fortress down was no small feat. Now transfer this image of medieval fortresses to strongholds in your mind. These are the fortresses that Satan seeks to erect in your thinking in order to do his dirty work. He erects these thoughts, often based on past traumas, media, or negative life experiences, which can lead to low self-esteem, a victim mentality, helplessness, guilt, pride, and more. Once the fortresses are built, the enemy uses them to launch further attacks against your mind as well as to repel your attempts to dislodge him. They can then become a self-fulfilling prophecy, or cyclical, as your actions then validate your thoughts, which then lead to more thoughts of the same kind.

One reason strongholds are so powerful is that they are so entrenched. They become entrenched when Satan can get you to buy into the lie that your situation is hopeless. His goal is to get you to believe that by nature you are a drug addict or a manipulator or a negative person, that you are controlled by fear or shame, that nothing will ever change, and so on. Once you give in to and adopt this line of thinking, the entrenched fortresses become difficult to remove. Your behavior deteriorates even more because we always act according to who we believe we are.

The only solution is to tear down these fortresses by "taking every thought captive to the obedience of Christ" (2 Corinthians 10:5). Reprogram your mind and release yourself from captivity. This is how you unleash your full potential and free yourself up to then help other men rise to do the same.

The solution is twofold but straightforward. First, identify Christ's thoughts on a matter, and secondly, align your own thinking under the rule of His truth. The truth, then, will set you free (John 8:32).

Keep in mind that just acknowledging the truth won't break any bonds. John 8:32 says that you "will know" the truth and then be set free. The word for "will know" is *ginosko*, a verb that literally means both "to know" and "to be known."[3] It is the same word used in Matthew 1:25 (NKJV) when the Scripture says that Joseph did not *know* (have sexual relations with) Mary while she was pregnant. The NASB says that he "kept her a virgin [*kai ou ginosko*] until she gave birth to a Son; and he called His name Jesus." The literal translation of *kai ou ginosko* in Matthew 1:25 is "and was not knowing her."[4]

To know the truth, in the biblical form of this word, is to make it an intrinsic part of who you are. It is to know and be known by it, in the deepest, most authentic place in you. It is to let the truth be as Hebrews 4:12 states: "Living and active and sharper than any two-edged sword, and piercing as far as the division of soul and spirit, of both joints and marrow, and able to judge the thoughts and intentions of the heart." You must meditate on, memorize, consider, abide with, and be continually engaged with God's Word for it to transform you and set you free. John 15:7 gives us this powerful principle in one sentence:

> "If you abide in Me, and My words abide in you, ask whatever you wish, and it will be done for you."

The "whatever" Jesus is talking about includes overcoming addictive behavior and self-defeating cycles. Your freedom to fully unleash the power of biblical manhood can be found in that solitary verse. Let Christ's words abide in you as you abide in Him. Without this abiding identity in Christ and His perspective on a matter, you will be bound by Satan's schemes. He will cut you short of reaching your destiny.

Yet when Christ's thoughts and His Word are released to dominate your soul, you will hold your head high and declare, like Everett, despite any difficulties you might face, "I am free."

I opened this chapter by telling you about a personal stronghold I had to overcome—the stronghold of workaholism. But that's not the only challenge I've faced. I've faced many over my seventy years, as I'm sure you have as well. Growing up in the era of the civil rights movement and the new Jim Crow caused me to wrestle with a confluence of emotions as anyone would at that time, and many still do to this day. I've had emotional struggles I needed to face and overcome, such as resentment, bitterness, and hopelessness.

I remember looking out my window as a teenager during the riots just after Martin Luther King Jr. was assassinated. I stood there staring at all the National Guard members, fully armed, who lined the streets. It looked like a war zone. I remember seeing them and fully feeling the anger present in many of us during that time of curfews and heightened security. I felt conflicted because I was dealing with a reality that could only be summarized as painful. These men had been called on and positioned there to do their job. But their job was to keep people like me in our homes. It was confusing and shaming in many ways, especially in light of the reality that "people like me" had just lost one of our greatest peaceful voices for civil rights through the violence of an assassination.

But at the same time, I was wrestling through the training I had received from my father. My father never wasted his words. "Love your enemy, Tony," he would say. He explained that you didn't have to love what they did, but you had to love them. You could hate the sin but love the sinner.

Growing up, I had to balance all of this within me emotionally. Struggling through this season led me to a life principle I've applied ever since: Faith must overrule everything, even my feelings. I learned that I had to operate on what I believed, not what I felt. I had to make my decisions based on the truth of God's Word, causing me to do what was right rather than allow my emotions to encourage me to do something wrong.

So on that day as I stared out the window as a black teenager in a city with streets lined by soldiers, I asked my dad if I could take them something to drink. I asked if I could take them some water. It was my way of putting feet to my faith. It was my way of demonstrating grace and kindness in the midst of confusion and chaos. It was my step in seeking not to succumb to the vitriol that the cultural environment called for, even though it was based on legitimate pain, but to rise above it.

Yes, my pain was real. The injustices were real. The killing of a peaceful leader who was helping us move forward as a nation cut deep. But I chose to respond in truth rather than react with emotion, based on the Word of God.

I've tried to carry that principle with me throughout my life since then. This does not mean endorsing the wrong. We are to condemn what is wrong. Yet, at the same time, we are to rise above it so we do not become trapped in a stronghold of bitterness or pain. Let me give you an example of how this played out in everyday life later on.

I'll never forget the time a man came in to do some work on our house. Everything was going fine until the man, who was white, called me "boy." At that very moment, all of my history rose up to the point of threatening to boil over. I just turned toward him with a glare. I'm black. He was white. He was using a term of denigration based on the past. What's even worse is that I was older than he. And a pastor.

All of that was hitting my emotions at the same time. I wanted to respond out of my feelings, but I decided to pause instead, based on this principle I learned as a teenager. I decided to whisper a quick prayer asking God to give me wisdom because I wanted to address the situation appropriately. Men, it's always a good thing to pause and pray when you don't know what to do. It could be that your emotions are responding without all the information. Ask God for wisdom.

I'm glad I did, because after a few moments a white man came in who was also around my age. The gentleman also called him "boy." Apparently, using this term was his habit, and he was unaware of the cultural context and how it might be offensive to me. Seeing him call the white man "boy" changed the whole atmosphere, because at first, I had taken it personally. But when I got more information, I better understood his intent.

Giving people the benefit of the doubt as you address emotional strongholds will also give you time to process what you are experiencing and the best way to respond. Waiting to learn intent can also de-escalate situations that might otherwise turn hostile. My concern is that if we remain so sensitive about anything that can cause an offense, driving ourselves more deeply toward "cancel culture" before examining the heart, we'll never move forward. We've got to learn to push pause and discern, question, and speak truth in love. Let the person know that what he or she did or said offended you and then ask them if they meant it or if it just came out wrong. Minister through grace. We all need grace at some time or another. I'm not saying we aren't to correct people who intend to offend or who offend out of a naïve lack of awareness. But kingdom men seek to discern first, before speaking and correcting in love.

Far too often our own emotions get in between us and God's carrying out His vengeance on someone who is doing wrong. It's like a basketball player who shoves another player with an elbow only to be shoved back and now the second man is penalized. Had he not responded wrongly, the foul would have been called on the first player. Override emotional challenges with patience and grace, responding with love, and in so doing you will open the door for God to intervene in a powerful way on your behalf. I've seen this take place in my life more times than I can even count. God is on your side. He just wants to make sure you are on His as well. You can show Him you are by how you choose to face and get over the challenges and strongholds in your life.

> Kingdom men seek to discern first, before speaking and correcting in love.

SEVEN

GET GOING

Nothing less than hate-filled revenge coursed through the veins of every man, throbbing strongly with every beat of their bitter hearts. They had not forgotten the brutal slaughter they had succumbed to years before. It had been Moses' last known battle in his quest for the promised land. Historic. Vicious. Unrestrained.

With a fierceness inflamed by the loss of twenty-four thousand Israelites[1] due to a plague brought on through deception, Moses had led his men into what can only be described as an all-out annihilation. Moses followed God's instructions to "be hostile" very literally. We read the instructions given to him in Numbers 25 as we set the stage:

> "Be hostile to the Midianites and strike them; for they have been hostile to you with their tricks, with which they have deceived you in the affair of Peor and in the affair of Cozbi, the daughter of the leader of Midian, their sister who was slain on the day of the plague because of Peor."
>
> vv. 17–18

Hostile doesn't adequately describe what happened next. Moses would charge his men into what could be called the Midianite Massacre, claiming upward of 100,000 lives, many of whom were women and children. This brutal battle sliced through the land like an oversized sword, severing generational lines of legacy in an instant. The result was a devastated group of people who had been completely pillaged and brought to ruin. Spoils for the Israelites included more than half a million sheep, 72,000 cattle, 61,000 donkeys, and 32,000 of the virgin women who had been spared from death (Numbers 31). All others lay dead.

Over two hundred and fifty years had passed since this torturous moment in time for the Midianites. But their memories remained just as fresh as the blood that once oozed from every sword-pierced man, woman, and child. Time hadn't let them forget. But time had given them the chance to rebuild and get stronger.

Thus, when we read in Judges 6 that Israel's own spiritual devolution into a culture of debauchery led to the ultimate consequence of God's wrath, it's not surprising that this wrath would come at the hands of the vengeful Midianites. They stood hungry—no, starving—on the precipice of retaliation. All God had to do was say the word, and they were unleashed upon the Israelites.

For seven years, Midian reigned down terror on their enemies like oversized hail crashing hard onto anyone and anything in its path. They forced the Israelites away from the farmland and pastures to live like refugees in caves tucked away in the mountains. As if to taunt them, they allowed them to till the ground just enough to grow a small harvest. Then they would rush in like a tidal wave in order to consume or destroy it, leaving the Israelites to starve once again.

Time and time again the Midianites descended upon the Israelites' livestock like locusts famished from one too many years underground. They left no sheep, no donkeys, and no oxen at the Israelites' disposal. The Midianites had one goal in mind: revenge. Scripture says they "came into the land to devastate it" (Judges 6:5).

The next verse can almost go without saying, but I'll share it because it helps put into place more pieces of the principles we're about to study. "So Israel was brought very low because of Midian, and the sons of Israel cried to the LORD" (v. 6).

You don't say? They called out to God in their despair. I'm not surprised. Hunger, fear, danger, assault, and thievery will bring any nation to her knees. Difficulties will do that. Hardship has a way of keeping people down and able to look up only for help. Yet despite the peril that seemed to confuse them, God had a purpose for their pain.

The stubbornness of their hearts had set them on a path of an indulgence-based cycle of defeat. These were God's chosen people, and He had a better plan for them than their own self-destruction. But through their rebellious choices, they had gotten off track from His divine plan. We see both the cause and the consequence of their choices a few verses earlier where we read,

> And the land was undisturbed for forty years. Then the sons of Israel did what was evil in the sight of the LORD; and the LORD gave them into the hands of Midian seven years. The power of Midian prevailed against Israel.
>
> Judges 5:31–6:2

After this recent period of respite, prosperity, and peace—Israel chose to turn from God rather than toward Him. They had drifted into the pursuit of narcissistic pleasures and privilege. Instead of serving God from a heart of gratitude, they wanted more. The last forty years of peace produced little more than puffed-up people drunk on their own personal power and pride. Here we have the cause. Thus, God gave them over to the hungry hands of the Midianites in order to remind them who they truly were. Here we have the consequence.

The Israelites' own choices led to their dire state of distress. God allowed the consequences to play out because He wanted them to learn from their sins.

See, one of the reasons God will either allow or create a crisis is to force our return to Him. When our departure leads to living out of alignment with God's will, God will often permit difficulties to happen, which will get us back on track. Now, we can return voluntarily, of course. We always have that option. Unfortunately, few of us usually do. Thus, when we insist on remaining apart from God in our thoughts, words, and actions, God allows circumstances to guide us back to Him. At times these circumstances are minor. Other times they are anything but.

Enter the Angel of the Lord

Frightened and famished, huddling in caves in the mountains, Israel had gotten a wake-up call of epic proportions. As a result, they did what anyone would do when being woken from a violent nightmare— they cried out for help. I'm sure you've done that before too. I know I have. You are fast asleep, dreaming, only to have your dream take one too many wrong turns. Before you know it, you're sitting up in bed and yelling for help, only to discover there's nothing going on in your dark room at all. It'll make you feel like a fool! But Israel's cry wasn't due to a dream, or even a nightmare. Israel cried out to God for their very lives. They begged Him to deliver them from the enemy breathing down their necks.

Yet unlike a soothing parent comforting a child from a frightful and bad dream, God responded with severe scolding instead. God didn't say, "There, there, my favored people, calm down. I'm here now." No, instead we read what seem to be the frustrated words of a holy God restraining himself through the mouthpiece of a prophet:

> The LORD sent a prophet to the sons of Israel, and he said to them, "Thus says the LORD, the God of Israel, 'It was I who brought you up from Egypt and brought you out from the house of slavery. I delivered you from the hands of the Egyptians and from the hands of all your oppressors, and dispossessed them before you and gave you their land, and I said to you, "I am the LORD your God; you shall not fear the gods of the Amorites in whose land you live. But you have not obeyed Me.""
>
> Judges 6:8–10

Before giving them a solution, God reminded them why they were there in the first place. He didn't want the lesson lost in His divine deliverance. God wanted the Israelites to remember what had caused this mess to begin with. In summary, He said,

I brought you up from Egypt.
I brought you out of slavery.

I delivered you from your oppressors.
I dispossessed others before you.
I gave you the land.
I am the Lord your God who did all these things and more.
But you have not obeyed me.

Despite all He had done for them, they had chosen to chase after idols like a dog after a stick. The gods of the Amorites had become their snare. A generation of entitlement and peace had led to a lifestyle of luxury and greed. The Israelites had neglected to honor God through obedience, so their own choices led to their pain, to scarcity, and to the struggles they now faced. By the way, in case you haven't picked up on it yet, God doesn't take idolatry lightly.

Following His straightforward summation of why they were crying out to Him, God then moved to the solution. It would be an unusual solution. But these were unusual times.

To start, God sent an angel of the Lord to a man busy beating wheat in a winepress. Yes, you heard me right. There was a man beating wheat in a winepress. If you wonder why he was doing it there, the answer comes in the history we just reviewed. He was trying to hide the wheat from the Midianites. Remember, they would come in and raid the food. In order to have anything to eat, the men had to get creative. Sneaky. Quiet. And be on guard at all times.

While beating the wheat, this man heard a voice. "The LORD is with you, O valiant warrior," said the angel of the Lord, who appeared to him (v. 12).

I'm sure the man looked up to see who had just spoken to him. Perhaps he even thought, *Did someone just call me a valiant warrior? Surely not.* Here he was, after all, hunched over wheat in a winepress, most likely glancing over his shoulder every so often to avoid being spotted. But the angel had called him a valiant warrior. And as the story will show, the title fit.

But the young man named Gideon didn't know that yet, so he didn't even acknowledge the grandiose title. It made little sense at that time. He just skipped right past it in his response. After all, he had more important things to ask anyway, things like the pervasive question of why. Why this? Why now? Why us? You can hear from him yourself:

> "O my lord, if the LORD is with us, why then has all this happened to us? And where are all His miracles which our fathers told us about, saying, 'Did not the LORD bring us up from Egypt?' But now the LORD has abandoned us and given us into the hand of Midian."
>
> v. 13

Gideon asked hard questions. And don't we at times do the same when things go wrong? "God, where are you and why have you allowed all of these problems in my life? Why am I going through all of this? Why didn't you stop that, change this, fix that, or solve this? Where are your miracles I've read about? Did you bring me here just to leave me to die? Look at how bad things have gotten, God."

That all-inclusive question, *Why?* I know I've asked *why* before. Many do. In fact, just a month after my wife had passed away from cancer, both of my daughters faced weighty health issues. My daughter Chrystal had an unknown growth in her leg, which doctors were exploring to discern how to treat it. And my daughter Priscilla had a severe irregularity on her lung, severe enough for the doctors to recommend that they remove an entire lobe. As a family, we had already suffered the loss of Lois, in addition to six additional deaths of close family members over the previous eighteen months. We were emotionally exhausted, depleted, and if I were to be brutally honest, confused.

As I sat with Priscilla in the hospital following a surgery so significant that they literally had to disconnect her lung from her heart to complete it, her eyes welled up with tears. "Why, Daddy?" she asked. "Why is all of this happening to us?"

Blurred by my own grief, I didn't have much more of an answer other than, "I don't know, Silla. I don't know." After a pause, I added, "But God does. We have to keep trusting Him." Life can do that to you sometimes. Life can take your own answers and understanding and kick them to the curb. Things don't make any sense at all. Maybe you've been there. I know I have. It's not a fun place to be.

Gideon must have been in this spot as well. I'm sure he had similar feelings as he stood in this sacred moment in time. He didn't care about being a valiant warrior right then. He just cared about his next meal. Life can get so rough so fast that even hope becomes a luxury. The first chance Gideon had to ask the question *why*, he took it. I can't blame him for doing just that.

But God knows what we need most in the midst of our struggle and pain. Thus, God chose not to answer Gideon's question of *why*, just as He often doesn't answer ours. Maybe it was because He had already answered it once through the prophet. Or it could be that He wanted to shift Gideon's focus off of yesterday and direct it toward tomorrow. Whatever the reason, we can learn some things from God's response. One is that, while there are times that warrant the asking—and we always have a right to ask—we must never demand an answer.

Another thing we learn is that it is not wise to allow the *why* to become a way of life. If you do, you could wind up stuck in a victim mind-set, which only pins you down. Far too many men forfeit a greater future because they remain chained to the pains of the past. Now, I understand that the things that happened back then may have been rough. They may have been unfair. But you can't change the past. No one can. You need to stop allowing your past to dominate your present and consequently destroy your future. Let it go, get up, and move on. A kingdom man entertains a question or two, from himself or those under his care, but then he goes forward to search for the solution.

Just Go

We see that the angel of the Lord's response to Gideon's questions of *why* skipped right over it with a charge: "Go in this your strength and deliver Israel from the hand of Midian. Have I not sent you?" (v. 14). A summary of the conversation could look like this:

Angel: "Hello, valiant warrior."

Gideon: "Why is my life so bad? Why is my nation in turmoil? Everything is a mess. God has left us on our own!"

Angel: "Go fix it."

The angel's reply boils down to one word. *Go.* Go simply means *to move, proceed—to head out in a certain direction.* It definitely doesn't mean to stay, remain, and vent about how bad things have been or are now. The angel responded to Gideon's cry for an answer with a command. And like a parent, for emphasis he added, "Have I not sent you?" In other words, do something about the problem.

But as we often do at times, Gideon remained confused. He pushed back with even more questions and concerns:

How can I go?
Who am I to do anything?
My family is unimportant.
I'm the youngest son of an unimportant family.

Essentially, he said, "Pick someone else. This is too big for me." Obviously, Gideon didn't want to go. His response reveals that. But God wasn't about to hear it. He had told Gideon to go, so He sought to strengthen him to help him do so. He assured Gideon that he would not be going alone. "Surely I will be with you," the angel of the Lord voiced clearly, "and you shall defeat Midian as one man" (v. 16).

Gideon needed the reminder that with God, your lineage, standing, and position don't matter. All that matters is who goes with you. It's a simple spiritual point but one we often gloss over to our own detriment. The key to accomplishing any impossible task is the presence of the Lord with you. It doesn't depend on your expertise or lack thereof. It doesn't even depend on your strength. Your strategy is no match for God's, so you might as well table it and follow Him. Spiritual success in spiritual war depends entirely upon spiritual solutions. Spiritual solutions take place if, and when, God goes before you or with you. That determines your outcome. We see this principle play out time and again in Scripture:

> Then he said to Him, "If Your presence does not go with us, do not lead us up from here."
>
> Exodus 33:15

"The LORD is the one who goes ahead of you; He will be with you. He will not fail you or forsake you. Do not fear or be dismayed."

Deuteronomy 31:8

"I will go before you and make the rough places smooth; I will shatter the doors of bronze and cut through their iron bars."

Isaiah 45:2

"It shall be, when you hear the sound of marching in the tops of the balsam trees, then you shall act promptly, for then the LORD will have gone out before you to strike the army of the Philistines."

2 Samuel 5:24

God either needs to go before you or with you to overcome the enemy at hand. His presence is your power. His wisdom secures your win. And remember, it's always okay to ask for confirmation on something as important as that. Gideon did, thus demonstrating that valiant warriors know their own limits. Gideon didn't want to go out to face the Midianites on his own. But he also knew that if God went with him, they could take the enemy down.

The Baal Fighter

So Gideon asked God for a sign, one of many signs he would ask for over time. But this first sign involved an offering he had made of meat, broth, and unleavened bread. After laying them on the rock, he poured the broth on top. We read what happened next:

> Then the angel of the LORD put out the end of the staff that was in his hand and touched the meat and the unleavened bread; and fire sprang up from the rock and consumed the meat and the unleavened bread. Then the angel of the LORD vanished from his sight.
>
> Judges 6:21

If the Lord consumed the offering, Gideon would know for certain with whom he had been talking. Which is exactly what happened. The passage continues,

When Gideon saw that he was the angel of the LORD, he said, "Alas, O Lord GOD! For now I have seen the angel of the LORD face to face." The LORD said to him, "Peace to you, do not fear; you shall not die." Then Gideon built an altar there to the LORD and named it The LORD is Peace. To this day it is still in Ophrah of the Abiezrites.

vv. 22–24

The Lord is Peace. That's quite a name for an altar during a time of bloodshed and war. Yet when God is present, even in times of madness, peace exists. Satan is the master of confusion and chaos. But God's presence always ushers in peace. That's one determinant you can use as you seek God's leading in your own life. He gives you pockets of peace when you are in alignment with Him.

After the offer and the answer, the Lord spoke again to Gideon with the instructions he needed to carry out the attack. He was to start by removing the idols from his own home. That's right—the victory for the nation began with one man. We read in verses 25–27,

Now on the same night the LORD said to him, "Take your father's bull and a second bull seven years old, and pull down the altar of Baal which belongs to your father, and cut down the Asherah that is beside it; and build an altar to the LORD your God on the top of this stronghold in an orderly manner, and take a second bull and offer a burnt offering with the wood of the Asherah which you shall cut down." Then Gideon took ten men of his servants and did as the LORD had spoken to him; and because he was too afraid of his father's household and the men of the city to do it by day, he did it by night.

As we saw earlier, idolatry had so permeated the culture that it was rampant by this point. Which is why this was the first thing God needed to address. The worship of foreign gods and foreign values had become so broad that even Gideon's father had an idol of Baal and an idol of Ashtareth in his house.

Thus, God instructed Gideon to remove the idols because before He would lead Gideon to fight the enemy outside of the camp, he had to extract the enemy within. The principle for us today as kingdom men is that we should not expect God to do something through us outside of our home or inner circle if we are not first willing to get things right within it.

You may have heard me say it like this: A messed-up man contributes to a messed-up family, which then contributes to a messed-up church. A messed-up church contributes to a messed-up community, which then contributes to a messed-up county. A messed-up county contributes to a messed-up state, which then contributes to a messed-up country. And a messed-up country contributes to a messed-up world.

> We should not expect God to do something through us outside of our home or inner circle if we are not first willing to get things right within it.

Therefore, if you want a better world comprising better countries made up of better states containing better counties populated by better communities housing better churches attended by better families, it starts off with being a better man. It starts with you. Right now. Right here. Just like the deliverance of the entire nation of Israel from the hands of the Midianites started with Gideon, in his own home.

God had raised up Gideon for a mighty conquest. But prior to taking him there, He asked him to be obedient with what he had around him. Matthew 13:12 phrases the kingdom principle like this: "For whoever has, to him more shall be given, and he will have an abundance; but whoever does not have, even what he has shall be taken away from him."

Faithfulness with what you have right now and right where you are is always the first step toward further use in God's kingdom. We saw this in the life of Shamgar in *Kingdom Man*. If you haven't read it, I'd encourage you to get that book and pay close attention to the chapter on Shamgar. God wants to see if you are willing to follow Him right where you are. He wants to know what you are willing to do right now at your pad—with your family and friends and even in your neighborhood and church. Don't waste your time on visions of grandeur if you are not willing to begin by addressing the sins that pervade within.

Gideon heard God's command and took action. He set out to win the national war by gathering ten men to go tear down the altars in his own home. Now, if it takes ten men to tear down some altars, these are not things that had been sitting on the mantel. These idols were a major presence in their family and in their home. Taking these down would not go unnoticed. Gideon knew that. That's why, to avoid any immediate objection or opposition, he and the ten men took the idols down at night (v. 27).

This truth raises an important point. While God provides pockets of peace in moments of uncertainty, our humanity leaves us vulnerable to ongoing emotional changes based on what we've been tasked with. Obedience as a kingdom man isn't always couched in calm. Sometimes that obedience takes place in a mixture of emotions. There is no doubt that Gideon was scared if he was traipsing around at night to pull down the family altars. But courage does not mean the absence of fear. Courage means right actions taken in spite of fear's presence.

There's nothing courageous about doing something you know will succeed without any opposition. Courage occurs when you rise up to do the task that looks impossible.

Gideon knew that tearing these idols down would not sit well with some. In fact, we read in verse 30 that, as a result, the men of the city called for Gideon to be killed. That shows just how strongly idolatry had become ingrained in the Israelite culture by that point. The very people of God wanted to kill the person who tore down the idols in the name of the living God. Gideon's father cleverly quelled the angry mob through both a question and a statement. He said,

> "Will you contend for Baal, or will you deliver him? Whoever will plead for him shall be put to death by morning. If he is a god, let him contend for himself, because someone has torn down his altar."
>
> v. 31

Joash, Gideon's father, made a strong case. If Baal is the god they say he is, shouldn't he be able to stand up for himself? If he's so powerful, why do mere humans need to defend him? His retort quieted the crowd and allowed their rage to subside.

In the midst of all that commotion, Gideon not only gained some much-needed courage, but he also gained a new name. His father named him Jerubbaal, meaning "let Baal contend against him" (v. 32). He got this name because he had successfully taken down the idols.

Gideon was now known as the Baal fighter. He had shown himself strong, and his reputation spread swiftly. In addressing the sin within Gideon's family line, God had simultaneously created a scenario that established his notoriety and reputation. It didn't take long for word on the street to get around. The youngest child in an unrenowned family whose life was threatened had become the Baal fighter overnight. All he needed to do next was blow a trumpet and send a message throughout Manasseh, and men would come running to support him in battle (v. 34). Why am I bringing up this fast turnaround? Because when God is ready to move, He can move quickly. *Suddenly.* It's a word used throughout Scripture when God swoops in and changes things on a dime.

I understand that it can be frustrating when circumstances don't appear to be in your favor. Or during those times when you want to be the person you know you can be but things haven't fallen in line. It can take a toll on anyone's patience when dreams rise up within you but life seems to be solely about surviving each day. You know you were made for more. You know you can accomplish more. But you are stuck beating wheat in a winepress.

If this is you right now, I want to remind you that even though waiting can be frustrating, know that when God decides to move He can shift the landscape overnight. I've seen Him do it in my own life numbers of times. I've also seen Him do it for others. When God is ready, it doesn't take long. He can turn a servant in a field into a Baal fighter leading the charge to freedom for a whole nation. He did it for Gideon, and He can do it for you.

Three Hundred Men Will Do

After Gideon got the call to command the troops, he asked God for another confirmation. Most of you have heard the story of Gideon and his two fleeces, how he asked God to ensure he heard Him right. Essentially, he prayed and asked for a sign. Twice. Which is exactly what we are to do as kingdom men. The reason you pray is because you are never to limit yourself to the processes you know about or are used to. Prayer is inviting God into the process to lead it.

Gideon needed to know he was hearing from God because God's processes are often strange, or I could use the word *weird*, to us. They aren't the normal approaches we would take.

Unfortunately, though, oftentimes when God leads many of us to pursue something, we often assume the processes and approach to take based on our own knowledge, skills, and understanding. We operate in the normative ways that have worked for us in the past. But God rarely works according to our strategies and plans. In fact, nothing will make God more real to you than those times when He overrides humanity's known processes to bring about a victory in your life.

So Gideon asked God for confirmation, again. After Gideon got his signs, he decided it was time to get going. The next part of the process is one of the most remarkable events in all of Scripture. I want us to read it in its entirety so we don't miss any of it. You might be familiar with the story, but I encourage you to read it again because you might see something new.

> Then Jerubbaal (that is, Gideon) and all the people who were with him, rose early and camped beside the spring of Harod; and the camp of Midian was on the north side of them by the hill of Moreh in the valley.
>
> The LORD said to Gideon, "The people who are with you are too many for Me to give Midian into their hands, for Israel would become boastful, saying, 'My own power has delivered me.' Now therefore come, proclaim in the hearing of the people, saying, 'Whoever is afraid and trembling, let him return and depart from Mount Gilead.'" So, 22,000 people returned, but 10,000 remained.
>
> Then the LORD said to Gideon, "The people are still too many; bring them down to the water and I will test them for you there. Therefore it shall be that he of whom I say to you, 'This one shall go with you,' he shall go with you; but everyone of whom I say to you, 'This one shall not go with you,' he shall not go.'" So he brought the people down to the water. And

the LORD said to Gideon, "You shall separate everyone who laps the water with his tongue as a dog laps, as well as everyone who kneels to drink." Now the number of those who lapped, putting their hand to their mouth, was 300 men; but all the rest of the people kneeled to drink water. The LORD said to Gideon, "I will deliver you with the 300 men who lapped and will give the Midianites into your hands; so let all the other people go, each man to his home." So the 300 men took the people's provisions and their trumpets into their hands. And Gideon sent all the other men of Israel, each to his tent, but retained the 300 men; and the camp of Midian was below him in the valley.

Judges 7:1–8

The Baal fighter learned through this that God doesn't mess around when it comes to spiritual battle. God wasted no time in making it known who was in charge. Gideon had rounded up 32,000 men to defeat the opposition. He had logically assumed that a big enemy requires a big army to fight it. Most men would assume that. But God set him straight, and fast.

What's more, He told Gideon why He did it: "For Israel would become boastful, saying, 'My own power has delivered me.'" This wasn't God's first rodeo. He wasn't about to allow His glory to be usurped by those He saved once again. To accomplish that, He had Gideon send 22,000 of his men home.

Even so, 10,000 men could still boast that the victory was all about them, so God whittled down the group even more. He strategically chose the 300 who demonstrated battle savvy. The 300 who lapped the water had positioned themselves to be on the alert. The remaining 9,700 who knelt down to drink were not wise enough to recognize their own vulnerability in war.

This was an important battle, so God chose the men who would rise up and be prepared to achieve victory. He didn't want the men who were just along for a quest to gain perceived glory. Thus, following the drinking of the water, Gideon sent all but 300 men home.

Now, you can probably imagine how Gideon was feeling right about then. The night before he had slept comfortably in his bed knowing that an army of 32,000 would have a good chance of winning. Especially if those 32,000 had God on their side. But now God had completely stripped him of his own tools, leaving him with an army of 300 to go up against bloodthirsty, vengeful combatants "as numerous as locusts" (v. 12). No doubt Gideon was fearful once again.

Knowing this, God sought to encourage him. He told Gideon to go down to the camp where the enemy now slept. God also knew that Gideon was so afraid that he wouldn't want to go alone. That's why He even told him to take his servant with him (vv. 9–10). Gideon was probably shaking inside by now. He might have been trembling. But despite his doubts, he chose to go to the camp. He would soon discover the trip was worth it.

Once Gideon got there, God allowed him to overhear a conversation about a dream one of the enemy soldiers had.

> And he said, "Behold, I had a dream; a loaf of barley bread was tumbling into the camp of Midian, and it came to the tent and struck it so that it fell, and turned it upside down so that the tent lay flat." His friend replied, "This is nothing less than the sword of Gideon the son of Joash, a man of Israel; God has given Midian and all the camp into his hand."
>
> vv. 13–14

When Gideon heard this dream, it instantly calmed his fears. He knew God had directed him to go down there to hear just that. Gideon's response was to bow in worship before God. Keep in mind, a barley loaf was poor man's food in that day. It's what impoverished people ate. Thus, a loaf of barley rolling down a hill into the Midian camp to destroy it perfectly symbolized Gideon's station in life. The dream hadn't been about a huge military conquest. No, it was a single loaf overtaking a swarm of well-armed soldiers. This dream may have also reminded Gideon of what the angel had said to him earlier: "You shall defeat Midian as one man" (Judges 6:16). Gideon had heard the word, and he knew that he was the one.

God will often use personal synchronicities to confirm and build upon what He has shared with you. We need to learn to pay close attention to God because He can use the most inconsequential events to make a serious statement. Particularly when you need assurance and courage due to your own hesitancies or lack of confidence in yourself, the strategy, or both.

After Gideon received his assurance, he commanded his men to rise up, "for the LORD has given the camp of Midian into your hands" (7:15). Gideon had once again found his strength in the Lord. He now wasted no time at all. With the courage of a champion, Gideon had his three hundred men divide into groups, march through the woods, blow their trumpets, and rout the enemy. Scripture says,

> When they blew 300 trumpets, the LORD set the sword of one against another even throughout the whole army; and the army fled as far as Beth-shittah toward Zererah, as far as the edge of Abel-meholah, by Tabbath.
>
> v. 22

The Midianites were startled out of their sleep, and the confusion caused chaos in the enemy camp. Some fled. Others warred against each other, killing their own. Then Gideon unleashed the men of Israel from various tribes to pursue those who fled, capture their leaders, and finish the victory that began with three hundred. Well, three hundred plus God.

Thus, God used Gideon and his army to obtain the freedom from oppression they so desperately needed. God brought that about because Gideon was willing to do what God said, even when it didn't make sense.

Part of rising up as a kingdom man involves doing what God says when it doesn't make sense. As long as the way you think God is leading you doesn't contradict His revealed principles in His Word, and you have received confirmation from Him to get going, you are to go. Your response to His leading often plays a larger role in the outcome than the strategy itself.

Nothing and no one can override God when He sets His mind on victory.

When God is ready to move, it doesn't matter how big your enemy is. It doesn't matter how entrenched the opposition is or how shattered your world has become. Nothing and no one can override God when He sets His mind on victory.

Kingdom men exist today in the midst of a pagan nation, on many levels. We are living in our own sort of Midian. We are sorely outnumbered as disciples in the body of Christ. The secular world has not only abandoned God, but it has taken up the offensive against the one true God. It is oppressing the church and the truth of Scripture in many ways. This is our cultural reality whether we like it or not. We can pretend it doesn't exist, but it does.

But it doesn't take millions to take ground back for Christ. In fact, three hundred will do. Gideon demonstrated that as he led his charge in the dark night. Similarly, we are to rise up and get going to do what God has called each of us to do so that we might advance His kingdom agenda on earth.

We must do this personally, and we must also do this collectively. If we sit around waiting for a majority, we will have waited too long. God knows how to handle the issues we face. It's our role to repent of our sins, clean up our own homes, trust God, and then do what He says. A few kingdom men in the hands of one mighty God can rout any evil that opposes them. It's time—no, it's past time—that we get going.

EIGHT

GET ALONG

When I was young, my father worked long, hard hours as a longshoreman on the harbor in Baltimore. As a black man without a diploma raising a family in urban America, his work options were limited.

Sometimes the work at the docks was unpredictable. Longshoremen often had extended periods without any work due to layoffs, strikes, or a lack of ships coming in. But during those times, I never saw my father sitting idle. He was a jack of all trades, repairing anything that anyone needed fixed in a makeshift shop in our basement. In fact, before my father got saved, he even brewed brandy in that basement to sell it as well.

The family atmosphere I knew was similar to the community I lived in. It was a functioning, relationally oriented, and stable community. People shared food and struggles with each other. You could tell they had a genuine care for each other. We didn't have much by way of material goods or opportunity, but we had a community governed by a moral code of mutual respect and personal responsibility in spite of segregation and poverty.

The trajectory of my life was influenced by relationships established during these young years. One person who stands out is the white business owner of Jewish descent whom I mentioned briefly in chapter 1. Martin Resnick hired me when I was sixteen years old to work at his company washing dishes. He would later tell me that he saw great potential in me because I was always on time, stayed late if needed, worked diligently, and then came to him to ask for more to do if I finished washing before my shift ended. As a result, he quickly promoted me to the position of personal chauffeur for his kids. In fact, it was he who encouraged me to go to college and even offered to pay for it himself if I would come back and work as a manager in his business. That's how I was able to leave Baltimore for Atlanta to attend Carver Bible College.

God had called me into ministry just prior to my first year of college, though, and by my second year I had earned several academic scholarships. Thus, my friend and mentor Martin wound up paying for my freshman year only. Regardless, it was his desire and willingness to proactively reach across racial lines that afforded me an opportunity and exposure I did not have on my own. This made a profound difference not only for me, but for my entire family line ever since. As you might imagine, Martin and I have remained close friends to this day.

When I was in Baltimore not too long ago, I spent some time with Martin at his home. Toward the end of the day, I began to thank him for the opportunities he had given me to know him and experience his belief in me. I thanked him for investing in me to such a degree that he helped show me a way to go further than I ever could have on my own. But as I was thanking him, he stopped me abruptly in my tracks. He wouldn't let me continue. Reaching for my hand, he said, "Tony, it's just the opposite. I've gained so much from knowing you—from watching you grow. To see what you have accomplished in your life and to see the meaningful way you have affected so many other people's lives, and then somehow you feel you have to tell me that I'm a part of that? No, it's the opposite. You have filled me with such pleasure and joy.

"In fact, I have tears in my eyes, and I hate to do this to you, to cry like this," he said, wiping his eyes and starting to get self-conscious, "but it's only because I am so proud of you. I'm so thankful that God gave me the privilege and the opportunity to be a part of your life. To be a part of your family."

One of the reasons I share this intimate look into my life is that it is a powerful example of what intentional, authentic relationships can produce. Whether they are cross-cultural, cross-class, cross-racial, or even within a person's own ethnic and class demographic, when we come together to help each other, both men win. When you set out to under-gird the legacies of others you simultaneously wind up strengthening your own heart, mind, and reach for impact. Legacy isn't only about what you personally leave behind. Your legacy also includes the influence and impact of the legacies of the men, or women, you helped to rise.

I also share this story to give you a peek into the social construct in which I and many others were raised. As a high school student in the 1960s, I couldn't get enough of the Bible. As an African American, my view was being formed in the reality of racial inequality. This caused me to focus on questions about race, oneness, and social justice in church history. I pored over the Scriptures to shed light on these issues, look-ing not only to the theology, but also to the practical application of that theology in everyday life.

This led to a quest for understanding, which produced my doctoral dissertation, "A Biblical Critique of Selective Issues in Black Theology." Later I wrote several smaller booklets on the subject, such as *Let's Get to Know Each Other* and *Are Blacks Spiritually Inferior to Whites?* and then ultimately my magnum opus on the topic, *Oneness Embraced*.

The truths I learned through those decades of study and searching apply to all races with regard to getting along in the body of Christ. Our unity is critical. We cannot advance God's kingdom if we cannot first learn how to get along. The failure in the church has resulted in the failure in society. We have failed to come together in any meaningful manner, and as a result, we remain divided as a nation.

A Peek at My Personal Experiences

My father was a key voice in pointing me to clarity during this time of confusion. I grew up just a few hours away from our nation's Liberty Bell, which so proudly declares, "Proclaim liberty throughout all the land unto all the inhabitants thereof," from Leviticus 25:10 (KJV). Yet, when I would go to a fast-food restaurant, I was denied the freedom to eat in a public dining room because I was black. The restaurant was pleased to take my money at the takeout window, but eating in wasn't allowed. Though I didn't fully understand it at the time, the contradiction between proclaiming liberty while simultaneously denying it shaped my mind. Thank God for my father, who knew what I was facing and who went to tremendous lengths to counteract the lie.

"Son," he would say, "you're a child of the King. If they don't want royal blood in their restaurant, then don't go in there." You can see how my earthly father pointed me to the truth of my heavenly Father. In this way, he seeded in me a vision for what it means to be a kingdom man in a secular land.

This is why it is so important, particularly for minority men, that we seek to communicate truth that cultivates character in the next generation. Solely pointing out to them the divisions and hatred that exist in our culture can actually harm their self-esteem and confidence. While it's never good to ignore reality, how you speak about it and what you choose to focus on will leave a significant imprint on those in your care. My father could have emphasized to me whatever he wanted. He chose to emphasize that I should focus on my true value and identity in Christ. He chose to mold me into a kingdom man.

I share these experiences with you to help those who are unaware of the things that many of us in minority communities face, and thus what many of us feel. I understand that there exist seismic gaps in our understanding of each other's history, when speaking of the specific division between black and white Americans.

I also share this to let minority readers know that I take part in our collective pain. The things I say and write about on how to address the racial issues in our land are not said from lack of personal experience. I have experienced racism on a multitude of levels. Which is why I want it rightly solved at its root and not just placated in unending approaches designed only to address the fruit.

I know what it's like to be stopped by the police and asked what I'm doing in a specific neighborhood. I have experienced this a number of times. I know the feeling of getting off work at an overnight job while in seminary, only to be pulled over because I'm driving home at night. When I was in college in Atlanta and I attended a white church with my white professor, I was told that I was not welcome there. Lois and I have been turned away from attending white churches as well, once even left standing at the door.

In fact, when I first attempted to broadcast my sermons on the radio in the late 1970s, the radio stations would not even carry my messages. And they weren't shy to say why. The only station that did was a small station in Houston, KHCB. I mention KHCB and its president, Bruce Munsterman, because I want to highlight that there have been all along, and still are, good people fighting racism and culturalism. The other stations all turned me down because they said a black man would offend their white listeners. It wasn't until a highly influential white Christian leader intervened by making phone calls and sending a letter to each of the stations, imploring them to change their ways, that a few stations began to open their doors. There are many stories I could tell you to show that I understand what's going on.

But what I don't want to miss in the personal stories is what allowed those stories to take place. They all happened because the Christian church itself had allowed its own internal systems of discrimination to remain strong. These systems did nothing to curb injustice but rather perpetuated the personal experiences of it for each of us as African Americans in our land.

Preserve Unity

The racial divide in our nation emanates from a theological issue first, not a sociological reality. Second Chronicles 15:3–6 tells us that due to the Israelites' departure from God, there was no peace in the land. They did not experience peace because, Scripture says, "God troubled them with every kind of distress" (v. 6). Now, if God is your problem, only God is your solution. It doesn't matter how many marches you have, what programs you create, how many protests you organize, or how many societal adjustments you make, because if the spiritual root is not repented of and fixed, any progress will last little longer than a chorus of "Kumbaya."

The only reason this problem has run this deep for this long is due to the failure of the church. Because the church, both leadership and members, has failed to come together, we have experienced continual spiritual setbacks in our culture. Had the evangelical leaders—some of them men we often celebrate—not endorsed slavery, along with Jim Crow, segregation, and many of the other systemic inequities present not only in our nation but also in our churches, this problem would not have lasted so long.

The reason we haven't solved the race problem in America after hundreds of years is that people apart from God are trying to create unity, while people under God who already have unity are not living out the unity we possess (Ephesians 4:3). Unless kingdom-minded Christians significantly enter the fray and become leaders in resolving the race crisis, we will be hopelessly deadlocked in a sea of relativity regarding this issue, resulting in restating more questions rather than providing permanent answers. It's only when believers willingly step out and put biblical theology concerning issues such as injustice, unity, and reconciliation on display—not just through words—that we can set a different tone and create a divine reset.

Until we see ourselves, and each other, as God sees us and respond by intentionally embracing His call of oneness, we will forever, like the cracked Liberty Bell, ring flat in a world that longs to hear the liberating cadence of truth.

Extract the Toxins

As I write this book, we are facing two simultaneous pandemics: a medical pandemic and a cultural pandemic. Yet, deeper still and at the root of both of these is a spiritual pandemic.

We have wandered far from the value system established by God for how human beings are to live, act, and relate to one another. Across racial and class lines we have come up with our own standards for how we treat each other, and it has not done us any good.

God has been known to allow chaos in order to create in His people a heartfelt call to Him for help. When we appeal to Him according to His kingdom rule, He is then able to reintroduce himself into the scenario and usher in the healing we so desperately need. Sometimes it takes a mess to make a miracle.

Everyone knows what it's like to suffer for a long time from stomach pains and then throw up and feel better relatively quickly. The throwing up is a messy situation, but the reason you feel better afterward is that you have purged the toxins.

There are a lot of toxins in our culture today. We have toxins of injustice, toxins of racism, and toxins of hate. We have a multiplicity of toxins coagulating in the same space at the same time. But if we miss the reality that God has allowed disorder in order to bring about a correction and a cleaning, then we will just move from one symptom to another symptom. We will miss the opportunity to address the root that has produced the fruit that has led to the confusion of hopelessness on display. The root of the problems we face in our nation today are clearly spiritual. It's only when we identify and understand the spiritual components that we are then able to translate them to the pragmatic realities of the cultural crisis at hand.

One of the roots for the chaos in our land is clearly the sin of racism. Racism isn't a bad habit. It isn't a mistake. It is sin. The answer is not sociology, it's theology. Spiritual leaders need to be just as bold in speaking out against the sin of racism as other sins. Individuals in the body of Christ must first examine their own hearts for areas of racism, resentment, anger, bitterness, pride, and other sins. Keep in mind, Scripture speaks of two types of sin. There are sins of commission (doing an action of sin) and sins of omission (failing to perform an action of righteousness). As James explains the latter, "Therefore, to one who knows the right thing to do and does not do it, to him it is sin" (James 4:17).

And based on Micah 6:8 alone, we all know the right things to do ("He has told you, O man, what is good"). For example, when someone says to me, "I'm not racist," I am glad to hear they feel that way and I do hope it's true. But Micah 6:8 isn't about not doing injustice. It isn't about not being a racist, either, to put it in context with our contemporary conversation.

Micah 6:8 doesn't call us to love justice. Neither does it call us to affirm justice. This passage specifically calls us to *do* justice. The word *do* is an active verb in the present tense. It requires action. Not being racist is wonderful, and I'm thankful for all who aren't. But the Bible calls us to more than that. According to the Word of God, we are to actively "do justice." One way is through opposing all forms of sin rooted in injustice, particularly those that hold others made in the image of God, *imago dei*, in an oppressed situation. It is equally wrong to refuse to forgive and reconcile with those who repent of their evil (Matthew 6:14–15).

I've never heard the argument on the pro-life side, "I'm not having an abortion," as someone's stand. Everyone knows that is not enough to save lives or combat this evil in our land. Scripture calls us to "open your mouth for . . . the rights of all the unfortunate" (Proverbs 31:8). We are commanded to do something to right the wrongs and eradicate the injustices in our homes, churches, communities, and land.

God has spoken on the issues at hand, and He has not stuttered. He has spoken about racism. He has spoken about systemic and individual injustices. He has spoken about classism. He has spoken about culturalism. He has spoken about equity, elitism, empathy, and more. Just read the book of James. That's a great place to start to learn. God has spoken about all of these subjects, but until we align our hearts, thoughts, words, and actions underneath His overarching rule, we are living in sin.

What many people do today, unfortunately, is pick and choose what they will obey. As a result, we are experiencing a dearth of kingdom men who choose to observe all that God has commanded, not just the parts they like. God is not going to bless a church, country, or culture that comes up with its own set of rules and asks Him to bless it. God has set in stone two rules to govern all we do. They are righteousness and justice, grounded in love.

Righteousness and Justice

We began this book by looking at God's choosing of Abraham—His drafting of him, so to speak—to make a great man and an even greater kingdom through him (Genesis 18:18). With this choosing of Abraham, God established two critical aspects of how His rule was to be made manifest on earth. Let's take a closer look at the next verse:

> "For I have chosen him, so that he may command his children and his household after him to keep the way of the LORD by doing righteousness

and justice, so that the LORD may bring upon Abraham what He has spoken about him."

Genesis 18:19

From God's throne come both righteousness and justice. It's not one or the other. It's both. In fact, righteousness and justice serve as the very foundation of His throne. We looked at the importance of foundations in chapter 3. We saw that if we get the foundation wrong, all else that is built on it will fall when the storms surge. Scripture says,

Righteousness and justice are the foundation of Your throne; lovingkindness and truth go before You.

Psalm 89:14

Righteousness and justice are not a seesaw to go up and down on. Rather, these are twins joined at the hip. You don't skip justice and call for righteousness. Likewise, you don't skip righteousness in the name of justice.

Righteousness is the moral standard of right and wrong to which God holds people accountable based on His divine standard. *Justice* is the equitable and impartial application of God's moral law in society.

God desires and requires His kingdom men to juxtapose both in our daily lives. God wants to protect the life of the unborn in the womb, but He also wants to see the justice for life once born, to the tomb. In other words, God wants a whole-life agenda and not a term agenda. But unfortunately, all lives aren't valued the same way in our country right now, even though they ought to be because every person is created in the image of almighty God.

Churches need to come together across racial and cultural lines to work toward the pursuit of both righteousness and justice in our land. We must speak out against, as well as work to undo, both individual and systemic injustices while simultaneously seeking to build up our families, neighborhoods, and communities through an emphasis on right living and personal responsibility. Working together to influence culture with a kingdom world view will make an impact. But until we become kingdom minded and not denominationally, racially, or class minded, we will not be Christ minded. Until we are Christ minded, we will not be socially minded to address the divisions between us and their resultant propagation of sin.

> Until we become kingdom minded and not denominationally, racially, or class minded, we will not be Christ minded.

Which brings me to a frequent retort I hear when societal ills, racial division, and biblical justice come up. What my white friends, and even pastors, have often said is "What this situation needs is the gospel!" This statement is made to indicate that we "all bleed red under the cross," and if, somehow, we would just preach the gospel of Jesus Christ, these problems would dissipate and be solved.

I couldn't agree more.

We desperately need the gospel. The gospel *is* the all-encompassing solution to the racial disparities in our land that breed division and chaos. The part I would like to add, though, is that we must preach and live out the whole gospel, and not just a portion of it.

The Gospel and Getting Along

Confusion exists today concerning the implications of the gospel and to what degree the gospel includes this mandate of justice. Some Christians believe that to include social liberation and justice in the gospel is to preach a different gospel. Others believe that to exclude social liberation and justice as part of the gospel is to deny the gospel. Liberation theology was formed on this latter thesis.

To resolve this dilemma, we need to make a distinction between the gospel's content and its scope. By determining this distinction, we can discover to what extent we are to "do justice" as the church as part of our comprehensive responsibility of proclaiming the gospel.

The content of the gospel message is limited and contained. Paul made this unmistakably clear in 1 Corinthians when he said,

Now I make known to you, brethren, the gospel which I preached to you, which also you received, in which also you stand, by which also you are saved, if you hold fast the word which I preached to you, unless you believed in vain. For I delivered to you as of first importance what I also received, that Christ died for our sins according to the Scriptures, and that He was buried, and that He was raised on the third day according to the Scriptures.

1 Corinthians 15:1–4

Clearly, the content of the gospel message is the death, burial, and resurrection of Jesus Christ. Scripture is plain that it is personal faith in the finished work of Christ that brings people the forgiveness of sin, a personal relationship with God, and eternal life.

The gospel's scope, however, reaches further into sanctification, within which are located the concepts of justice and social action. We see this scope in Paul's use of the word *gospel* when he informs the Christians in Rome that by the "gospel" they are established (Romans 16:25). Likewise, in the book of Romans the gospel is called "the power of God for salvation" (1:16) and is said to include "the righteousness of God . . . revealed from faith to faith" (1:17). This righteousness includes sanctification, since "the righteous man shall live by faith" (Romans 1:17; see Habakkuk 2:4).

In addition, the gospel is viewed as the criterion of Christian conduct (Philippians 1:27), and believers are viewed as being obedient to the gospel when they are active in the ministry of love to poorer believers (2 Corinthians 9:12–13). Paul further exemplified that the gospel involves more than the preliminary reception of salvation, but also a life of liberty, freedom, and multiracial relationships when he rebuked Peter for drawing distinctions between Gentiles and Jews on the basis of race. Paul said that in doing so Peter had not been "straightforward about the truth of the gospel" (Galatians 2:14).

We read the context of this story in Galatians 2. Peter had crossed the railroad tracks after the Lord had instructed him to do so and he began relating to people of a different race and a different culture. In fact, he got into this so much that he started eating with Gentile believers in Antioch.

But that's exactly where the problem developed. Some of Peter's friends from the Jewish part of town in Jerusalem came down to Antioch. When they showed up, "he began to withdraw and hold himself aloof" from his Gentile brothers and sisters (v. 12).

Why did Peter do this? Because the Jews said, "Peter, what are you doing here eating with Gentiles? Don't you know we Jews don't do that? It's against the guidelines of our race. We'll all get together in heaven, but on earth we don't have that kind of social relationship with Gentiles." So Peter stopped having fellowship with the Gentiles because he feared what his Jewish brethren would say.

That's when it got really bad. "The rest of the Jews joined him in hypocrisy, with the result that even Barnabas was carried away by their hypocrisy" (v. 13). When Peter pushed his chair back from the table and left, so did the other Jews who had previously joined him. In fact, even Barnabas got caught up in it. Barnabas was raised in Cyprus, a Gentile colony. He was raised with Gentiles, went to school with Gentiles, and played with Gentiles. But that's how bad racial divides are. They can take a good man and make him act badly. So Barnabas followed Peter out the door.

There was only one problem: Paul saw it. Paul was equally committed to his Jewish history, culture, and people, yet he publicly excoriated Peter's non-Christian action, saying that Peter was "not straightforward about the truth of the gospel" (Galatians 2:14). The key point is truth. An objective standard transcended Peter's cultural commitment.

The fact that not even an apostle could get away with such an action is very instructional and should not be marginalized in its importance and contemporary application. No one is excused for placing culture above Christ or race above righteousness. God's standard reigns supreme, and cultural preferences are to be denounced publicly when a Christian fails to submit to God's standard. Scripture, and only Scripture, is the final authority by which racial relationships are determined.

Paul did what he needed to do. As a kingdom man, he held another man accountable for unrighteous and unjust behavior. He called him out by saying, in my paraphrase, "Peter, you are messing with the gospel. Stop it!" Having caved in to the racial pressure and prejudice of his fellow Jews, Peter had failed the test of truth. He had left the Gentiles in order to not offend the Jews. In deference to the cultural pressure of his own race, he discredited the message of the gospel that God had so graphically conveyed to him in the home of Cornelius (Acts 10).

Why did Paul hold Peter accountable publicly? Because he saw that Peter and his Jewish pals "were not straightforward about the truth of the gospel." That's the kingdom solution to divisions that exist in the body of Christ along class, cultural, racial, and even denominational lines: Be committed to the truth. He then reminded Peter of his identity in Christ (Galatians 2:20). This should be the posture of every kingdom man, if we are going to heal our racial divide.

The gospel also encompasses the whole man as directly stated by Paul elsewhere, "Now may the God of peace Himself sanctify you entirely; and may your spirit and soul and body be preserved complete" (1 Thessalonians 5:23). A view of mankind that divides the invisible world (soul) from the visible world (body) narrows the understanding of the scope of the gospel. This is reflected in a desire to save people's souls, thus compartmentalizing a section of man; that is, saving an aspect of man as opposed to the man himself.

This division between the immaterial and material parts of man leads to a lack of application of biblical justice through emphasizing the spiritual over the social. However, the soul and the body are to be seen as a unified whole. Biblical terms referring to the spiritual aspects of man support this reference to man's whole person, including the body. The Hebrew word for soul, *nephesh*, refers to the whole person, which includes the body (see Genesis 2:7; Lamentations 3:24). In the New Testament, the Greek word for soul, *psuche*, is used to refer to Christ's body, seeing as souls do not die and go to the grave (Acts 2:27).

Therefore, the church is commissioned to deliver the content of the gospel (evangelism) so that people come into a personal relationship with God. Yet the church is also commissioned to live out the scope of the gospel (sanctification) so that people can realize the full manifestation of it in their lives. The content of the gospel produces oneness in the church as we evangelize the world together. The scope also produces oneness through good works that are based on the principles of biblical justice (see Micah 6:8).

Unity isn't just about getting along; it's about getting things done. We'll never experience a movement of kingdom men rising in our nation until we have kingdom men relating to each other in the body of Christ in an authentic, mutually honoring manner. Racial reconciliation isn't about playing a video of an ethnic preacher to your white church on Sunday, or vice versa, or even reading *White Fragility* or *Oneness Embraced* and posting that you did so online. While those things are good, they—in and of themselves—are not unity. Unity takes place when people join together with oneness of purpose. It is working together in harmony toward a shared vision and goal. Unity involves doing justice together, not just talking about it.

Oneness Does Not Mean Sameness[1]

Unity is not uniformity either. Nor is it sameness. Just as the Godhead is made up of three distinct persons—the Father, the Son, and the Holy Spirit—each unique in personhood and yet at the same time one in essence, unity reflects a oneness that does not negate individuality. Unity does not mean everyone needs to be like everyone else. God's creative variety is replete, displaying itself through a humanity crafted in different shapes, colors, and styles. Each of us, in one way or another, is unique.

> Unity occurs when we combine our unique strengths and skills as we head toward a common goal.

Unity occurs when we combine our unique strengths and skills as we head toward a common goal. It is the sense that the thing we are gathered for and moving toward is bigger than our individual preferences. Our common goal is ushering in the manifestation of God's overarching kingdom rule on earth.

Submission to God's kingdom rule opens up this flow of heaven's involvement in our lives and in history. Far too many of us as men are satisfied with the part of Christianity that takes us to heaven, but not the part that brings a bit of heaven down to earth. But in order to bring to earth what "is in heaven," God's will must be done. Jesus' model prayer, the Lord's Prayer in Matthew 6:9–13, reflects this as well, and Jesus states He was to be solely about His Father's business (see Luke 2:49 KJV). Since Christ is our example, we should be about the same.

One of the elements of God's rule and His "business" is His heart for oneness. So important is the issue of oneness in the family of God that we are told to look out for people who seek to undermine it (Romans 16:17). In fact, God promised to judge those who divide His church (1 Corinthians 3:17). This is because God's kingdom followers are to reflect the values of the kingdom of God to a world in desperate need of experiencing Him.

The family of God is the only authentic cross-racial, cross-cultural, and cross-generational basis for oneness in existence. It is the only institution on earth obligated to live under God's authority while enabled to do so through His Spirit. In 1 Corinthians 12:12–13, Paul wrote,

> For even as the body is one and yet has many members, and all the members of the body, though they are many, are one body, so also is Christ. For by one Spirit we were all baptized into one body, whether Jews or Greeks, whether slaves or free, and we were all made to drink of one Spirit.

The baptism of the Spirit at the moment of salvation, the act whereby God places us into the body of Christ, secures the oneness God wants us to have. This inimitable work of the Spirit positions us under the rule of God. The Greek word for *baptism* used in the Bible means "identification." It was used of a cloth maker dipping cloth into dye so that the cloth would take on the color of the dye. The cloth was then said to be baptized, or identified, with the dye.

When we got saved, we were baptized into the body of Christ. We are now identified with a new family, having been placed into a new spiritual environment while still on earth. No matter what our race, gender, or class, when we came to Jesus Christ we entered into God's oneness because we came under His authority.

That is why Ephesians 4:3 says that we are to "preserve the unity of the Spirit." The Scripture uses the word *preserve*, indicating that we don't create unity. Authentic unity, then, cannot be mandated or manufactured. This is so because God desires that His standards alone serve as the basis, criteria, and foundation for oneness. It is also why He thwarts attempts at unity that ignore or exclude Him (Genesis 11:1–9).

The church has already been given unity because we've been made part of the same family. Although biological families don't always act like families, as believers we have access to family relationships because we are all adopted by God through the presence and power of the Holy Spirit.

A perfect example of spiritual unity came on the day of Pentecost when God's people spoke with other tongues (Acts 2:4). When the Holy Spirit showed up, people spoke in languages they didn't know so that people from a variety of backgrounds could unite under the cross of Jesus Christ. The people who heard the apostles speak on the day of Pentecost were from all over the world, representing at least sixteen different geographical areas, racial categories, and ethnic groups (Acts 2:8–11). But in spite of the great diversity, they found true oneness in the presence of the Holy Spirit.

We see the manifestation when the Holy Spirit moved like a "violent rushing wind" and "filled the whole house where they were" (Acts 2:2) in the midst of the oneness of the believers on the day of Pentecost.

At the end of Acts 2, the presence and product of oneness is emphasized as we read "Everyone kept feeling a sense of awe; and many wonders and signs were taking place through the apostles. And all those who had believed were together and had all things in common" (Acts 2:43–44). Signs and wonders took place when they were together and "had all things in common." God manifested himself when they were one.

What made this place and this period so electric was that the spirit of God had taken over. The miracles that happened did not happen because the individuals had the best program, the best technology, or the biggest buildings in which to meet. They didn't have any of that. In fact, they barely had any income. No one among them had notoriety, a wall full of academic achievements, or charisma. They were simply common people bonded together by a common purpose across racial, class, and gender lines, thus receiving the Spirit's flow among them.

The Power of Unity

Unity brings with it many benefits. One is power. In fact, we see that even God recognizes how powerful oneness is when we read in Genesis 11 about the time when all of the people on the earth used the same language. They gathered together and decided to build a city with a tower that would reach into heaven.

God's response to what they were doing is recorded for us. He says, "Behold, they are one people, and they all have the same language. And this is what they began to do, and now nothing which they purpose to do will be impossible for them" (Genesis 11:6). God then confused their language and scattered them over the whole earth because He knew that oneness is powerful. Nothing expresses the power of oneness as much as this incident at Babel. If God recognizes its power and importance in history when it's embraced by unbelievers operating in rebellion against Him, then how much more important and powerful is it for us?

Jesus Christ placed a tremendous emphasis on His desire for us to be one as His followers just hours before He laid down His life for us. This isn't something He is asking us to do only during "Unity Month" or on "Cross-Cultural Sunday." This is a mandate from our Commander in Chief that we be one with Him (vertically) and, as a result, one with each other (horizontally).

Another benefit of living a life of unity as kingdom men is that, in doing so, we are rising up to let the world know about the King under whom we serve. Getting along in authentic unity brings glory to God by allowing us to experience God's response of fully manifesting His glory in history. All of the praying, preaching, worship, and Bible studies in the world can never bring about the fullest possible manifestation of God's presence like functioning in a spirit of unity in the body of Christ can (see John 17:1–26).

This is precisely why the subject was the core of Jesus' high priestly prayer. It was the core because it reveals God's glory unlike anything else. It does this while at the same time revealing an authentic connection between one another in the body of Christ, which serves as a testimony of our connection with Christ. Jesus says, "By this all men will know that you are My disciples, if you have love for one another" (John 13:35). Based on that verse alone, we must get along or we are failing as kingdom disciples. A third benefit of oneness is found in this Old Testament passage penned by David:

> Behold, how good and how pleasant it is for brothers to dwell together in unity! It is like the precious oil upon the head, coming down upon the beard, even Aaron's beard, coming down upon the edge of his robes. It is like the dew of Hermon coming down upon the mountains of Zion; for there the Lord commanded the blessing—life forever.
>
> Psalm 133:1–3

Unity is where the blessing of God rests, coming down from heaven to flow from the head to the body, and even reaching as far as the mountains of Zion. In other words, it covers everything. The reverse is also true: Where there is disunity, there is limited blessing and limited power. We cannot operate in disunity and expect the full manifestation and continuation of God's blessing in our lives. We cannot operate in disunity and expect to hear from heaven or expect God to answer our prayers in the way both we and He long for Him to do. Disunity—or an existence of separatism, from a spiritual perspective—is essentially self-defeating and self-limiting because it reduces the movement of God's power and blessings.

Jesus made it clear that a house divided against itself cannot stand. Whether it is your house, the church house, or the House of Representatives, division leads to destruction (Matthew 12:25). Not only that, but a spirit of dishonor can lead to this same destruction (1 Corinthians 12:22–26). Honor promotes unity while dishonor promotes division. Dishonor is not the same thing as disagreeing. A person can disagree with another person but do it in an honorable way. However, when dishonor is given to someone of a particular racial, social, or class background that has a history of the same, it negates attempts at unity.

Four Areas to Address

It is absolutely clear right now that we need a reset among us as men. It is now time, on a personal level and a systemic level, that we reverse the course of history that has brought us to this point and that we reverse it on *every* level. This is a defining moment for us as kingdom men. Will we rise together to change a narrative steeped in apathy, hate, and pride, or will we remain stagnantly separate, allowing the culture to continue to decline? If we are ever to fix this madness and solve this mess—on these issues of injustice, the pain of our shared history, and the systems that perpetuate inequity—it will only be due to a right response, collectively as His body, based on God's Word.

God has four distinct spheres in which life is to be lived, and therefore, there are four areas in which changes need to be made, according to His kingdom agenda.

This change begins with the **individual**. We cannot change the nation if we don't first allow God to change our hearts. We have to develop a heart that cares for our fellow men because they are created in the image of God. Not because they look like us or have what we have, but because they have the stamp of divine creation on them. And that means you have the responsibility to reach out to somebody different from you, to hear from them and build a relationship.

This individual transformation then must flow into the **family** as parents transfer these values to their children. We cannot expect people to think differently and act differently if they aren't hearing differently from their parents—if they aren't getting a righteous value system of judging people by the content of their character, not the color of their skin.

But this is only the first step; families must then make connections with other families who are different from them and should partner together to serve yet another family that is worse off than theirs. This is where reconciliation happens, not in seminars but in service.

Thirdly, the evangelical **church** needs to speak up where it has been silent on injustice and racism. The church must address racial, economic, healthcare, and opportunity inequity, as well as recognize the systems that work against the fair treatment of people. In doing so, they help to create opportunities for all to responsibly take advantage of all that God has blessed us with in this nation. We must further hold people accountable for their decision-making.

The church must also speak with one voice, emphasizing the kingdom of God rather than partisan politics and popular views. We have one God, one Lord Jesus Christ, and one inerrant Word to speak from. And yes, we should protest evil in a righteous way. We should let our voices be heard, but then we must act, because if we don't act, all we've done is given a speech. We must implement righteous principles, modeling them through the church, so the world can see what they look like in the broader society.

And then, finally, we must engage with and challenge our **civic leaders** in all levels of government to be agents of healing and not division and to speak in such a way that unity is reinforced and not divisiveness. We must demand that the words that come out of their mouths and the way they say those words be both strong and kind, not vitriolic and mean. Additionally, policies should represent God's standard for how civil government should function.

When those four areas—the individual, the family, the church, and the community—begin to operate based on God's standard for getting along, then He can feel comfortable to get back in the midst of us and make us repairers of the breach and healers of the land.

It is time to fervently pray and repent of where we fail to do what God says to do in the way He says to do it. We must ask God to realign us under His authority while pursuing a relationship with Him so that His Word can overrule our ideas, perspectives, and agendas.

Our current cultural season is a defining moment for us as men and as churches to decide whether we want to be one nation under God or a divided nation apart from God. If we don't answer that question correctly and if we don't answer it quickly, we won't be much of a nation at all.

PART THREE

TRANSFERRING BIBLICAL MANHOOD

NINE

SETTING THE STAGE

It started as a light rain. There was nothing unusual about it other than how long it lasted—which wasn't very long at all. Almost as quickly as it began, the drizzle turned into a downpour. Then, nearly as quickly, the downpour became a deluge. What had begun as a tropical wave off Africa's west coast just a few weeks earlier now pummeled southeast Texas like a sleep-deprived toddler throwing a tantrum.

They called him Harvey—Hurricane Harvey, that is. But 2017's Harvey was no nice elderly grandfather, as many of us imagine when we hear that name. No, Harvey grew into a high-strung, angry teenager terrorizing anyone and anything in his path. Harvey's rapid intensification brought storm surges, some as high as 12 feet, crashing uncontrollably onto land. Peak wind gusts topped 140 miles per hour.[1] Rain no longer fell, it flooded, breaking bridges and breaking records. The more than 60 inches of rain recorded in some parts of Texas topped any amount previously recorded in US history.[2]

Unlike Hurricane Katrina in 2005, which swept in and out quickly, leaving the broken levies to do the most damage, Harvey chose to hang around. In fact, Harvey remained in the Houston area for days—making it the longest tropical storm, up to that point, to linger in one general location. That it was stuck between two high-pressure systems, which were trying to push the storm in opposing directions, only led to further disaster. Harvey unleashed his fury on the southern parts of the state for four unrelenting days.[3]

To say that Harvey hit hard would be an understatement. Rather, Harvey raged.

Yet in the midst of one of the strongest, most destructive storms to rip through our nation, humanity responded with the restorative cohesion of grace. Stories of rescue and relief poured in, almost as unrelentingly as the rain. Neighbors helped neighbors. Strangers helped strangers. Churches helped churches. Businesses helped businesses. Pets were sheltered until owners could be found. It didn't matter what color, class, or political affiliation you were—humanity helped humanity when Harvey came to town. We witnessed devastation and restoration simultaneously. It was a display of unity at its greatest, reminding us that we truly are one race, composed of a variety of different ethnicities, made in the image of God (Acts 17:26).

No one bothered to check what color you were or label you claimed when calling out for or responding with help. One story that circulated widely at that time involved an elderly white couple rescued from their flooding home by employees of a nearby restaurant and one employee's African American neighbor. He had volunteered to go on a risky trek with his Jet Ski in order to rescue a stranger he had heard about only minutes earlier.

How an elderly couple got in touch with a restaurant during the middle of a hurricane to begin with is interesting in and of itself. Let me start there. First, for those of you who are not yet close to my age, some context will help. Most of you know that I'm a grandfather. My grandkids and great-grandkids call me Poppy. I don't always like to admit, or act, my age, but I am a Poppy and a Poppy will do what a Poppy will do.

For example, grandparents are known to try to pay less at a restaurant by using the senior discount. I've done that. And grandparents will often go to the same restaurant where the employees and managers have come to know them by name. I've done that too. In fact, there are many places here in Dallas where I can walk in and get a doughnut or a dinner, and I'm greeted with, "Would you like the regular, Pastor Evans?"

It's just what grandparents do. We have our routines. We enjoy familiar faces. We like to save money. There's nothing wrong with that.

In fact, this reality came in handy for J. C. Spencer and his wife during the hurricane.

J. C. was a regular at the local Chick-fil-A. The manager involved with the rescue was quoted as saying that J. C. would call every single day to order his breakfast or lunch. "Sometimes twice a day," manager Jeffrey Urban said in an interview. Jeffrey knew J. C.'s name and his number. As a manager of one of eighty Chick-fil-As in Harvey's path, Jeffrey had gone in to check on the damage.[4] He didn't take the time to pick up the phone when several calls came in, because he was focusing on the damage at hand. But when he saw a number he knew come across the screen, he couldn't let it go. It was the only call Jeffrey answered that day, but it would prove to be an important one. Their conversation went something like this:

"Jeffrey, it's J. C. I'd like to order two chicken burritos," he said, laughing nervously. J. C.'s wife, Karen, would later say they decided to call Chick-fil-A because they knew that emergency response centers would be too busy.

"Two chicken burritos, Mr. Spencer?" Jeffery asked, somewhat caught off guard.

"Yes, two chicken burritos," J. C. continued. "Oh, and a boat. Can you send a boat?"[5]

The manager understood right then and there what he had to do. He quickly called a co-worker, who joined with her neighbors to head over on a boat and some Jet Skis to rescue J. C. and his wife. They were picked up and ushered to safety in no time at all. You may have even seen the picture online of the Jet Ski heading out of the back door of a flooded home, with a black man and an elderly white woman both smiling at the camera. It was a photo shared by many because it appealed to something deep within each of us that desires to see humanity help each other in need.

Reflecting on that horrific day, redeemed by the kind sacrifice of others, J. C. later said, "This tragedy has made us stronger as individuals and as a family, and made Houston stronger as a community."[6] Coming together during difficult times will do that.

The flood ended up being disastrous for many, though. After the initial wave of rescues would come weeks, months, and years of cleanup.

Countless individuals and churches united to assist in the rebuilding and restoring of the southern parts of Texas that were hit the hardest. We were able to help, both as a church and as a national ministry, by providing materials, money, food, staff, and volunteers where we could.

Many other churches and communities sent volunteers from Texas and beyond. The restoration of the Houston area in the aftermath of Harvey was one of the strongest displays of working together across race, class, and cultural lines that we had seen in some time in our nation. It was a breath of fresh air in the midst of the stagnant fumes of division strangling us all for far too long.

Soldiers in a war don't care about the color of the person next to them, as long as they are shooting in the same direction. When individuals or communities face challenging circumstances, a unified approach to the solutions at hand must take place. *United we stand, divided we fall* is not just a catchphrase to post on social media or put on the bumper of your car. It's truth. Yet, as we are seeing through the cultural events unfolding more and more these days, without this truth and these values passed down to the next generations, we will face unending chaos and distress.

When men fail to transfer the faith, we wind up with a generation of young people who do not know the Lord, His heart, or His rule. Any culture disintegrates when worship turns away from God and toward idols. The idols might be money, power, prestige, or even education—but whatever it is, an idol holds no candle to God. It cannot save you when you need it most.

In addition, if and when God is no longer worshiped, God will do what He always did in Scripture and throughout history. He will back off. He will remove himself from the consequences brought on by the systematic marginalization of His presence.

When that happens, it won't matter what your title is, how much money you have, what your degrees are, the size of your house, the car you drive, or what you've accomplished. None of that will make a difference when chaos erupts. What good is a big house when the inhabitants in it are fighting? Similarly, what good is a house when the floods rise? Money can't buy safety. Peace isn't for sale. You can't buy purpose. You can't buy comfort. You can't even buy happiness, for that matter. These gifts come from the living God. Leave God out of the equation, and you leave these things behind as well.

That is why it is the responsibility of every kingdom man to remind every other person within his influence about the values of the kingdom of God. It's not just a good idea or a suggestion. This is our responsibility, men. This is what Abraham did when he had all the men in his household and employment circumcised. He was aligning them under God's kingdom covenant (Genesis 17:26–27). We are to do nothing less. Even if that means stepping out of your comfort zone and taking part in uncomfortable situations or uncomfortable conversations. Yes, you might wind up offending someone as you speak truth, but as long as you speak truth in love (Ephesians 4:15), that's on them, not on you.

Many of you probably saw former NFL player Emmanuel Acho's "Uncomfortable Conversations with a Black Man" video when it was first posted during the initial stages of 2020's onslaught of racial conflicts. The first video he put up had almost 2 million views last time I checked. I first saw it when he posted it that night because Emmanuel actually grew up in our church. In fact, his father—Dr. Sonny Acho—was on staff as one of our pastors for a number of years. The Achos were frequent guests in our home, as we were in theirs. Our kids hung out together and played backyard ball together, and we developed a family relationship over the years.

When I saw Emmanuel boldly posting his video addressing the "uncomfortable conversations" we were needing to have in our nation right then, I couldn't help but feel proud. That's what discipleship is. That's what transferring biblical values looks like. It involves your willingness to speak truth, as Emmanuel stepped out to do, even when truth may not be received well by everyone at that time. He was living out the manifestation of kingdom discipleship, front and center.

Now, when Emmanuel's second video came out around a week later, the one in which he sat down with actor Matthew McConaughey, and I heard my own words coming out of Emmanuel's mouth, I about picked up the phone to call and ask him for an attribution. No, I'm kidding. I just smiled, grateful to see spiritual truths spoken boldly on his platform. He said,

I think individually we must each fix the problem because I believe that individuals, they affect the houses; and the houses, they affect the cities; and the cities affect the states; and the states affect the nation; and the nation affects the continents. So individually, you have to acknowledge, "Maybe I do have a bias" and fix it.[7]

Hearing my heartbeat, illustration, and preaching come out through his words reinforced this belief I have in the power of discipleship. That video went on to get millions of views as well. That's what the transference of kingdom values looks like: Those who were once in your sphere of influence are now out there spreading biblical truths in their own spheres of influence.

Yes, it takes boldness. Uncomfortable conversations aren't easy. People don't always want to hear truth. Discipleship isn't necessarily fun. But neither are drills. Neither is conditioning. Yet all of that is necessary for any football team to achieve greatness. Similarly, discipleship is necessary for a kingdom man to both achieve and pass on greatness.

A kingdom man consistently seeks to transfer the values of the kingdom of God to those under his care, regardless of the openness or the response. We do this because we are pursuing the well-being of our families and their future and the well-being of the collective family of God. It is critical that we do this and that we do it regularly.

> A kingdom man consistently seeks to transfer the values of the kingdom of God to those under his care.

As a reminder, although it's obvious to most, when you remove conscience from a society, everyone is at risk. When people no longer care about themselves or anyone else, the culture is in jeopardy. The further you move away from God, the further you move away from conscience. The further you move away from conscience, the more dangerous things become. What's more, there is no politician in the world who can impose a law to legislate morality. The issues we face today in our nation are ethical, moral, and spiritual at their core. This is because when you leave God and His values out of the dialogue, discourse, and solutions, you create chaos.

Transferring kingdom values must take place on a regular basis through reminders and authentic conversations. It's not done only through seminars, books, or radio broadcasts. Those things are good, but they are supplemental. The transferring of kingdom values, as clearly outlined in Scripture, takes place person to person and heart to heart.

It Takes Both

We discover one example of this during a time of a different kind of flood. This wasn't a flood brought on by a hurricane or typhoon. This was a seasonal flood, and these can be devastating no matter where you are. Floods wreak havoc. They make ordinary tasks nearly impossible at times. Just imagine what they do to already difficult tasks like, for example, sending several million people across a river along with their livestock and weighted-down wagons piled high with possessions.

That's exactly what we read about in Joshua 3. You are probably familiar with the story, as it shows up often in preaching and teaching. When most people teach on this biblical example, however, they don't mention the water. But I feel it's important for us to keep an eye on the water in this situation. Because knowing that God told the Israelites to cross the river during flood season helps us better understand His purposes in our own paths as He guides us.

God didn't instruct them to cross during the dry months when the water was low. He didn't send them when the shores were more hardened. He didn't guide them to the narrowest part of the river after the sun had baked the clay either. No, God told them to cross the wide Jordan during the time they knew would be the most difficult to do that. We recognize it was flood season because it was the time of the harvest, and the banks of the Jordan River were high with water on both sides (Joshua 3:15).

God sent the entire nation across a river precisely when it was the most dangerous, fear-inducing, and impossible to cross. And He did this, as He does all things, intentionally.

God knew what the Israelites were about to face. He knew the battles ahead. He knew the culture of the people who were going to wage war against them. They were large people with even larger appetites. Appetites for blood, power, and violence. In fact, when the Israelites first spied on the land decades earlier, fearful reports came back that the enemies who lived in it were cannibals. Numbers 13:32 says, "The land through which we have gone, in spying it out, is a land that devours its inhabitants." The Hebrew word translated as "devours" is *akal*, which means to "feed on human flesh."[8]

The Israelites balked at that first report in Numbers 14, if you remember. As a result, they wound up wandering in the wilderness until the adult generation died out. It was the next generation who now stood on the precipice of promise, staring at a bloated river filled to the brim. They were about to cross *that*? Now? How? Worse yet, once they crossed, they had the cannibals in Canaan to fend off. God knew they needed their own miracle to feed their courage in the face of what was to come.

Difficulties can develop your faith muscles when responded to rightly. Moses' miracle at the Red Sea had become but a passed-down story to most of the men now staring at their own worrisome water and awaiting wars. Stories are good for temple services, campfires, or before going to sleep. But stories wouldn't carry these men through upcoming bloody battles. Stories wouldn't unify them across tribes when they needed to face their enemy as one. No, they needed to see God's hand for themselves. They needed to accomplish a victory together. They needed to step out in faith, literally, and wade into the waters. God knew that, which is why He sent them at this specific time.

Like a loving father, God focused on transferring the principles of kingdom living and biblical manhood to the current generation. Discipleship is a process whereby you and I partner with God in teaching those in our spheres of influence about the things He is doing in our lives and also in theirs. That's why maintaining a close, abiding relationship with God is so necessary, as well as open and authentic relationships with others.

Unfortunately, too often we expect those we influence—whether they are men we disciple, our adult children, teens, or those we serve with but who are younger in the faith—to simply hear what God has done for us.

Somehow we think our stories alone should build their faith. "God did it for us," we say. "See?" But kingdom discipleship doesn't work that way.

Transferring kingdom principles doesn't only happen in small group settings when we share about past adventures, although that is important. Life lessons often must be experienced by the individuals themselves in order to root deeply. Discipleship doesn't take place only through discourse. It comes through relationship, partnering, and doing life together. Yet it seems that we often get so focused on the pro forma group studies, weekly meetings, or programs that we have forgotten this truth. We have forgotten what actually accomplishes the outcomes we desire and so desperately need. After all, reading through the "Red Sea Miracle in Seven Weeks" study can only go so far. Especially when you are standing on a riverbank staring at a raging river you have been asked to cross with your family, livestock, and possessions.

God knew the Israelites needed more. He didn't march these men into upcoming battles with only the knowledge of what their parents and grandparents had experienced. He knew this generation needed to become personally familiar with His power. That's why He guided them into, and through, their own life lesson first. With the patience of a parent, God led the way. He started by telling them what He was doing and why He was doing it. Through Joshua, He said,

> "By *this* you shall know that the living God is among you, and that He will assuredly dispossess from before you the Canaanite, the Hittite, the Hivite, the Perizzite, the Girgashite, the Amorite, and the Jebusite."
>
> Joshua 3:10, emphasis added

By what? By *this*: Getting them across the Jordan River during flood season. By doing *this* impossible task. And what's more, God would then ask them to set up a marker after the miracle. We'll get to it in more detail later, but it involved the stacking of stones to serve as a conversation starter not only for them but also for future generations.

It takes both. It takes the stories of yesteryear's victories that are to be taught, shared, and listened to combined with the miracles of that very moment in order to provide the strength for spiritual success. When we expect those who come after us to wage their own victorious spiritual battles on the memories of our past triumphs alone, we are failing to fully equip them. It takes both the past lessons and the present learning. Discipleship is a partnering process of growth.

Take a Step. Grab a Stone.

Consider this: The Israelites had just spent forty years in the wilderness due to the previous generation's failures in faith. Forty is a significant number in the Bible. Jesus was in the desert for forty days prior to transitioning to public ministry. Moses was on the mountain for forty days before receiving the Ten Commandments. A generation is often referred to in terms of forty years. Forty involves this concept of transition. It was time for the Israelites to transition into the promised land, away from the futility of their yesterdays and into a greater tomorrow. They'd had forty years to be humbled, to have habits corrected, to be trained in truth, and to learn faith. Now they were being put to their first test.

The problem was their first test would be a big one. To get across this river would require two miracles, not just one. That's right. God would need to do more than one miracle to pull this off. First, He would need to stop the waters from flowing. Then, He would need to dry up the land. We read about His plan to do both in Joshua 3:12–13 and 17:

> Now then, take for yourselves twelve men from the tribes of Israel, one man for each tribe. It shall come about when the soles of the feet of the priests who carry the ark of the LORD, the Lord of all the earth, rest in the waters of the Jordan, the waters of the Jordan will be cut off, and the waters which are flowing down from above will stand in one heap. . . . And the priests who carried the ark of the covenant of the LORD stood firm on dry ground in the middle of the Jordan while all Israel crossed on dry ground, until all the nation had finished crossing the Jordan.

Two miracles in one lesson. Yet it all started with them. The reason the priests had to step into the water first is that before they could see what God would do, He wanted to see what they would do. Similarly,

God wants to see the same from you. Talking by faith doesn't mean much when it comes down to it. God wants to see you walking by faith. The priests demonstrated their trust by putting their feet in the water. Then, and only then, did God dry up the land. God is still waiting for men to take the first steps of faith.

Following the river crossing, God gave them their next move. It was in this context of supernatural intervention that He told Joshua, as the representative of the people, to do something very important to seed this life lesson even more firmly in their hearts and minds. Joshua was told to choose twelve men, who would also serve as representatives for each tribe of Israel, to pick up a stone from the middle of the Jordan River.

These men were to grab large stones from the area where the priests had stood while the Israelites crossed over. They were to then bring these stones with them, each to the location where they would later lodge (Joshua 4:3). Each man's stone was so large that he had to carry it on his shoulder (4:5). After everyone had reached the other side and settled into their camp on the eastern edge of Jericho, Joshua had the twelve stones assembled together at Gilgal (4:20). The miracle was memorialized with stones of remembrance. These stones were to set the stage for future victories by helping the Israelites visualize the past.

God did not want the Israelites to forget what He had done there for them. He didn't want them to forget where they came from and how they had gotten there. He had them set up a perpetual reminder that it was not by their might nor by their power that they had come this far. The twelve stacked stones solemnly declared that they were there because of the supernatural hand of God.

Maybe He did this because He had seen how quickly His people had forgotten the miracle of the ten plagues, the parting of the Red Sea, the food in the barren desert, and the water from a rock. He knew His people were prone to forgetfulness. So this time, He established a visible reminder of His sovereignty in the midst of humanity's struggles.

Remembering who God is and what He has done is critical for each of us too if we are to effectively transfer the principles of biblical manhood throughout the generations. That's one reason God emphasized this so much in Scripture. A few examples include the following (emphasis added):

> "Only give heed to yourself and keep your soul diligently, so that you *do not forget* the things which your eyes have seen and they do not depart from your heart all the days of your life; but make them known to your sons and your grandsons."
>
> Deuteronomy 4:9

> "Then it shall come about when the LORD your God brings you into the land which He swore to your fathers, Abraham, Isaac and Jacob, to give you, great and splendid cities which you did not build, and houses full of all good things which you did not fill, and hewn cisterns which you did not dig, vineyards and olive trees which you did not plant, and you eat and are satisfied, then *watch yourself*, that you *do not forget* the LORD who brought you from the land of Egypt, out of the house of slavery."
>
> Deuteronomy 6:10–12

> "Beware that you *do not forget* the LORD your God by not keeping His commandments and His ordinances and His statutes which I am commanding you today."
>
> Deuteronomy 8:11

> "Then your heart will become proud and *you will forget* the LORD your God who brought you out from the land of Egypt, out of the house of slavery."
>
> Deuteronomy 8:14

> "But *you shall remember* the LORD your God, for it is He who is giving you power to make wealth, that He may confirm His covenant which He swore to your fathers, as it is this day. It shall come about *if you ever forget* the LORD your God and go after other gods and serve them and worship them, I testify against you today that you will surely perish. Like the nations that the LORD makes to perish before you, so you shall perish; because you would not listen to the voice of the LORD your God."
>
> Deuteronomy 8:18–20

Do not forget.

You shall remember.

If you ever forget.

The references ring regularly throughout God's Word. I really like the phrase used in Deuteronomy 6:12 where He says, "Watch yourself." That sounds like a parent, doesn't it? "You need to watch yourself," or "Be careful not to get the big head," or "Check yourself." It's easy to forget that you're not all that and then some when things are going well or you just crossed a river in flood season. It's easy to think you are your own source. It's also easy to assume that everything you have is because of you. When you think that, you run the risk of also thinking it's now up to you to defend it, protect it, and preserve it any way you can when you feel threatened.

Yet God alone is our Source. He fed us in our own seasons of wilderness. He put shoes on us in the desert. He preserved us even when we were out of fellowship with Him. Truth be told, God has protected most of us from the damaging consequences of our own wrong choices countless times. None of us would even be here today if it weren't for God's merciful hand. God doesn't want us to forget that. He didn't want the Israelites to forget that either. Thus, He had them set up a memorial as a reminder of what He had done.

Talk about It

When I had the honor of filming *Kingdom Men Rising* at the NFL headquarters in New York a few years back, I was taken to a special area on one of the higher floors that housed all the Super Bowl rings. They also displayed the Lombardi Trophy in this room. It was a unique experience. Each ring sat carefully placed behind intricately crafted glass in a climate-controlled atmosphere. It was just NFL VP Troy Vincent, my wife, and me. It's hard to speak when you see so much history laid out before you. You just want to take it all in. So we all walked quietly through the museum-like room and looked closely.

The air was silent as we continued to stare at each date, each jewel, each emblem. Yet in the silence I began to hear the underpinning echoes of the victories represented by each ring. So many accomplishments clamored for my thoughts. So many wins. As I looked at each one, it struck me that this immaculately crafted ring didn't only reflect the one victory it was tied to. No, each ring reflected countless hours of weight-room pain, unending late nights studying game film, wins battled out during driving rain or under blazing sun. I considered the multiplicity of other personal sacrifices by players, parents, coaches, management, and even fans. Effort, commitment, and sheer grit had been poured into the mold to create each ring on display.

After we had taken a moment to absorb it all, we started to talk. Different rings led to conversations about different plays and players. What we saw turned into a rich dialogue about historical moments in sports lore. Memorials, awards, trophies, and other things of this nature often act as catalysts for communication. Joshua 4:6–7 explains it this way:

> "Let this be a sign among you, so that when your children ask later, saying, 'What do these stones mean to you?' then you shall say to them, 'Because the waters of the Jordan were cut off before the ark of the covenant of the LORD; when it crossed the Jordan, the waters of the Jordan were cut off.' So these stones shall become a memorial to the sons of Israel forever."

God knew that just setting up the stones of remembrance wouldn't be enough to transfer the truths learned during that event. The stones set the stage, but they didn't fill it. Filling the stage for the future narrative to take place would require more. That's why God explained to the Israelites the purpose of the stones. They were to be a conversation starter for discipleship to take place.

Psalm 145:4 says,

> One generation shall praise Your works to another, and shall declare Your mighty acts.

Here we have the blueprint for generational kingdom transfer:

Set up your marker to commemorate what God has done.

Talk about it with those under your influence.

Encourage them to experience their victories, set up their markers, and talk about them with those under their influence.

Repeat.

The cycle of generational transfer is an ongoing process if it is to work at all. A memorial is never enough on its own. We've all seen what happens to unattended memorials. They get overgrown with weeds. In fact, most of us don't even know why a lot of the memorials are there. Trophy cases often get stuffed to the brim, only to become covered in dust. Life goes on, and we forget to even look. Yet, kingdom men are to never forget what God has done. Kingdom men are to have a transferable faith through engaged communication, not just memorials, trophies, or stones stacked high.

Do you know why we are in cultural chaos? It's because there has been a transfer problem. We have a generation of young people who may have seen plenty of trophies or stones but have not had anyone sit with them and tell them what those stones and trophies mean. Why? Because the generation before them didn't transfer it. They just kept putting their trophies on a shelf.

We are facing a massive transfer failure because we have neglected to tell those under our care about what God has done in our lives. We have neglected to have the long conversations. The uncomfortable conversations. We have neglected to go into the specific details of lessons learned through failures of our own. Sure, we might have pointed at our miracle moments and said, "Look what God did." But that's not the same as taking the time for values transfer. As a result, we have failed to empower the generations after us to move forward into their own experience of God.

Consequently, we are living in a modern-day manifestation of Judges 2:10–12:

> All that generation also were gathered to their fathers; and there arose another generation after them who did not know the LORD, nor yet the work which He had done for Israel. Then the sons of Israel did evil in the sight of the LORD and served the Baals, and they forsook the LORD, the God of their fathers, who had brought them out of the land of Egypt, and followed other gods from among the gods of the peoples who were

around them, and bowed themselves down to them; thus they provoked the LORD to anger.

When a new generation stands on their own overflowing riverbank or faces their own floods of uncertainty, crisis, and fear, a stack of stones isn't enough. They will need more. They will need much more than "God did such-and-such for my dad," or "God did such-and-such for the men at my church," or "I think God may have done something way back when, but I'm not sure what exactly." They need to know that God is a God of the past, but He is also a God of right now.

That's why I love the name God shared with us when He first introduced himself to humanity. When Moses asked who He was, He answered swiftly, "I AM WHO I AM" (Exodus 3:14). God is not a trophy to be stuck somewhere out of sight. God is the God of this moment in time. He is the living, active God who leads and guides us. Each generation must be told about God regularly. That's how transference takes place.

But it can't stop there. Those you seek to transfer kingdom values to must also be encouraged to walk with God themselves and experience His hand themselves. That's how they, in turn, rise up as kingdom men.

Each kingdom man is to continually look for God in the present realities of life. We are to teach those who come behind us not to rely on our experiences alone but to learn from them and then walk into their own. We must never be content to hold up our own spiritual breakthroughs as if the existence of them is enough to leave an imprint. The transfer comes through the telling. That's how we pass on the kingdom principles of biblical manhood. We pass them on by continually talking about what God has done while simultaneously encouraging others to experience Him for themselves. Only then will there be something for the next generation to pass on as well.

Living Stones on the Stage

I had the gift of turning seventy years old not too long ago. Time caught up with me, and before I knew it, I was seventy. I don't feel seventy. At all. But the numbers on the calendar don't care how I feel.

Those who know me know that I'm not one to make a big deal out of much of anything, especially my birthday. But this time was different. Very different. Because of my late wife's battle with cancer, and because our birthdays fall fairly close together, when we had both turned seventy, our kids and our church put together a Sunday-morning birthday celebration service. It was wonderful. The musical guests brought life and dynamic singing. The tributes and speakers touched our hearts. But one thing happened that morning that will hold an extra special place in my spirit forever. It was a literal living manifestation of the stones of remembrance. Our kids had planned this as a surprise for us, to bless us and let us see the legacy and impact God had made through us in them.

As you can well imagine, it was very emotional for me. To see my children, their spouses, my grandchildren, and my great-grandchildren walk across the church stage, each holding a representative stone of their life, was powerful. Priscilla described what each stone said, which reflected the person holding it, as each person walked across the stage. She shared how it related to generational impact. After this, they all piled the stones in the center of the stage to serve as a visual reflection of a memorial. I now have them sitting on a table in the den of my home.

I wept as I watched them. I wept as I watched Lois watching them too. The reason I wept was that their lives highlighted that history had been made through us in them. Our love laid the foundation for a legacy of generations of kingdom faith.

As I sat there, I thought about Lois and how she had poured into me for almost fifty years and into us as a family. She made us her priority. The result of all her love and dedication now stood before us. Seeing them all walk across the stage one by one became a roller coaster ride of feelings. The sadness was there because of the late stage of Lois's illness, but there was also gratitude that God had favored me, and us, in this way. To see our family members honoring her, and us together, was something that mattered more to me than houses, money, cars, or notoriety. In that moment, I basked in the light of legacy.

Some of the younger grandkids and great-grandkids moved around on the stage or jumped up and down, not yet realizing the gravity of the moment, due to their age. It was fun to see them having fun. They may not have truly understood the magnitude of what they were doing right then. But they will one day. When they reach an age of greater awareness, they will be told. They will be shown. They will come to know the importance of the stones they held. Eventually, they will also tell their kids and grandkids. They will tell how the stone represented each life and our engagement in each of their lives. It spoke of our love for them, correction of them, pain with them, celebration with them, memories shared, conversations had, and dreams dreamt together.

These stones of remembrance will always rest heavily on my heart and in my mind. It's difficult to talk about it now or write about it even though so many months have passed. It's difficult because when I do, I begin to picture it and relive it. I picture each one walking across the stage from youngest to oldest, honoring us in this truly special way. No birthday cards were needed. No gifts necessary. Just stones. Stones representing the living legacies of our hearts, Lois's and mine.

This experience left an indelible imprint on my soul. This was truly one of the highlights of my life, and I will carry it with me for the rest of my days—just knowing that my family loves us as they do and loves the Lord as they do. Nothing could make me more grateful to God for the kindness He has given me by allowing me to witness the transference of kingdom principles to those I love so much. My family stood before me as the embodiment of the living stones Peter wrote of that were "being built up as a spiritual house for a holy priesthood" (1 Peter 2:5). My heart was full.

But while having your own family mature in the Lord and grow in their love for each other is rewarding, I realize that not everyone is in a position to experience this. Some come from broken homes. Others are single. Some of you reading this book may have already raised your families and made multiple mistakes along the way. Whatever the case or whatever the reason, this message of leaving memorials as a transfer of faith is for you too. It might not be to your family, but you could transfer it to those in your church as a leader or small-group facilitator. You could transfer kingdom values to others in your community. You can do it through serving, or friendships, or extended family. This is not a one-size-fits-all family-based formula for transferring the values of the kingdom of God, although it preferably starts there.

But if you can't do that due to circumstances, I want to embolden you to still take the premise of the principle, that of transferring the history of God's hand in your life through telling it to others, and then encouraging them to do the same. Whether it's with your family, friends, neighbors, social media followers, co-workers, or others, you are here as a kingdom man to transfer the values of God.

A Reputation of Strength

God gives us another reason for setting up the stones in the closing portion of Joshua 4. This marker was also to serve as a match to spread the story of what had happened to others so that "all the peoples of the earth may know that the hand of the LORD is mighty, so that you may fear the LORD your God forever" (Joshua 4:24). The memorial was not only to remind themselves and the next generation, producing a greater fear of God in their hearts, but it was also there to proclaim God's might to the world.

The Israelites were crossing over into the promised land. The problem in the promised land, though, was that it was full of evil. God wanted the Israelites to know that even though evil would surround them, He had them in His hand.

God also wanted the Canaanites, Hittites, Amorites, and others to hear the stories about what He had done for the Israelites. He wanted them to hear the miracles He had done in their midst. He chose to show off what He had done so their enemies would know His strength. That way they would gain a better idea of what, and whom, they were actually up against. In doing so, God set out to establish the reputation of the Israelites as a nation whose God was over all.

It is unfortunate that we have a generation rising up with few spiritual memorials being talked about in the transfer of the faith. We need to turn this around. We need to remember those times when God showed up and showed out, stepping into our situations to do something unreal. We are never to forget those times. Not only that, but we must be intentional about making these moments known to others.

After all, Red Seas don't open up every day. Jordan Rivers don't get stopped from flowing every day. Giants don't fall every day. But when they do, we need to ensure that we remember, that we tell the story regularly to others, and that we let the unbelieving world witness the power of our great God. When David killed Goliath, he took the giant's enormous sword and put it in his own tent. He did that for one reason. That sword served as a perpetual reminder that if any other nine-foot-six fool were to come against the people of the living God, he would meet the same end.

Similarly, kingdom men ought to be sharing about the transformation of lives, the marriages that were saved, the dignity that was restored, and the spiritual victories taking place. We are to transfer the experiences of God in our midst—small or large—through authentic relationships built on mutual trust.

It's worth noting that not only did Joshua set up the memorial at Gilgal, but he also assembled twelve stones in the middle of the Jordan, where the priests had once stood. These stones were to remain as a memorial underneath the water once it flowed again (see Joshua 4:9).

> When the waters are too high, the problems loom too large, and the needs threaten to crash like waves over the soul, God is there and able to handle it all.

The stones under the water remind us of something different entirely. They remind us that God does some of His best work in the flood seasons of our lives. When the waters are too high, the problems loom too large, and the needs threaten to crash like waves over the soul, God is there and able to handle it all.

When something is beyond your ability to get over or get through, it is never beyond God's. If something is beyond your capacity to pull off, remember that it is never beyond His. God can stop a river in flood season, deliver an elderly couple from a home in a hurricane, cause a once-paralyzed NFL player to dance again, make a lame man walk, give a golf course to a man who was once prohibited from playing on it due to his race, set free a former cocaine addict, and rout an entire army of enemies with just three hundred men. Whatever you are facing, it is not beyond God's ability to handle. I'm telling you that firsthand. But I don't want my stories to stop with me. Go and experience your own. Follow God with reckless abandon in a committed faith and see what He will do for you. Then challenge those within your sphere of influence to do so too. It is time for us as kingdom men to collectively rise to the level for which we have been created and called.

TEN

FURTHERING THE FUTURE

Four men sat nervously in the maternity waiting room back when men had to remain outside during the birth of their children. They tried to pass the time through casual conversation, barely paying attention to each other. Finally, the first nurse came in and said to the first father, "Sir, congratulations! You have twins!"

The father laughed and replied, "Wow, that's funny because I work for the Minnesota Twins!"

Another nurse came into the waiting room a bit later and said to the second father, "Congratulations—you have triplets!"

This father chuckled at the irony. "Really?" he asked. "That's great because I work for 3M."

The third nurse came out a bit later and said to father number three, "Congratulations, you are the proud and busy father of quadruplets!"

He broke out smiling and said, "That's ironic since I work for the Four Seasons."

The fourth father suddenly got a strange look on his face. The nurse and the third father turned to him and said, "What's wrong?"

"Oh," he replied, "I'm concerned." They asked why. To which he replied matter-of-factly, "Because I work for Seven Up!"

While this is obviously a joke meant to start a heavier chapter in a lighter way, the feeling of the story rings true. In fatherhood, as in any influential role, you can get more than you bargained for.

I'll never forget watching my son Jonathan adjust to the COVID-19 lockdown in Dallas. At that time, Jonathan and his wife, Kanika, had five children under the age of eleven. As you can imagine, when the mandatory shelter-in-place order went into effect, along with the closing down of all schools, Jonathan and Kanika had their hands full.

For Jonathan, juggling working full-time between the church and our national ministry, on top of fathering well by helping with school, entertainment, meals, and exercise day in and day out, week in and week out, was taxing. I could see the fatigue in his eyes at times. He was managing everything rightly, but it was a lot to manage.

So when the option became available for a certain number of staff to volunteer to work in the office rather than from home, I wasn't surprised when Jonathan's hand shot up first. Even a few hours at the office would provide some space to focus.

Jonathan is one of the best fathers I've seen, but the many responsibilities of parenting can take their toll, especially when piled on each other. As can the responsibilities of influencing others through discipleship, mentoring, and shaping the next generation. It's easy to raise your hand and say, "I need some space." And while personal space is critical for you to rest and recharge in order to remain healthy, opting out entirely due to the pressure, or a lack of commitment, is not. There's a difference between taking a break and bailing altogether.

Unfortunately, far too many of today's men have chosen to bail out on this charge of transferring kingdom values to others. They will either leave or simply become unavailable. Now, they may not always leave physically, but far too many men leave in other ways. They check out. They put in the headphones. Run to the gym or golf course, again—and again. They stay longer at the office than they need to or play video games. They turn up the podcasts. Whatever it looks like. They fail to engage, and remain engaged, which is one of the foundational components of effective discipleship.

As a result, our churches and our culture wind up suffering in a crisis of empty hearts, hopeless homes, barren neighborhoods, and broken communities. When you look around, you could even say that in many ways it looks like we are under a curse. The Bible makes it clear in the last verse of the book of Malachi that when men neglect their God-given calling to lead and love, the land is cursed (see Malachi 4:6). So we shouldn't be surprised by what we are seeing across the land.

It's obvious to most keen observers that much of what we face in our nation today comes from this lack of a responsible approach to values transfer. This is one reason why we have a generation rising up who are in many ways crippled and confused by their anxiety, anger, blame, hypersensitivities, and more.

I'm sure you've seen enough Olympic relay races where the dreams of the team came crashing to the ground simply due to a slip of the hand. Even though the team may have been out ahead of the others, their race abruptly halted when the baton dropped. An essential key to winning any relay involves the passing of the baton. It doesn't matter how fast a runner got out of the blocks or how fast he or she ran if they dropped what was in their hand.

Life is no different. You must pass on kingdom values in this race or it's game over for everyone. Being a kingdom man never stops with you. If it does, then you aren't a kingdom man at all. Faith is not a one-person race. A kingdom man leaves a legacy of a spiritual inheritance to others. Proverbs 13:22 puts it this way,

A good man leaves an inheritance to his children's children.

While this verse addresses fathers, the principle transcends roles. Each man needs to be, at a minimum, a three-generation thinker. This holds true whether it concerns your family, friends, or whomever you influence. Discipleship isn't a sprint relay. It's a marathon relay. And marathons are taxing. They are tiring. Runners have to build endurance just to race in a marathon and finish, let alone win.

One of the reasons we have so many men walking away from their responsibility to influence their families and the culture for good is because they have not learned to strategize for long-term gain. It could be that they gave too much too soon and burned out. Or they lost interest. Or maybe they bail when they don't see any immediate return on their investments in others. We live in such an instant-gratification culture that personal values like commitment and diligence are quickly waning. Yet whatever the challenges, we need more men willing to step up to, and stay in, the battle for biblical manhood.

A Father's Role

Now, before we transition to the broader principles for furthering the futures of those in your care, I want to give a refresher on biblical father-hood. While fatherhood is not the topic of this book, it is an important aspect of rising up as kingdom men. If you want to read more on the subject of parenting, I've listed a resource in the notes.[1]

In biblical culture, the job of raising children rested on the father, not the mother. The dad was vested with this main task. The mom helped fill in the gaps when the father couldn't be there. We see this as the normative instruction in Scripture. I'll give you a few examples:

> You [fathers] shall teach them diligently to your sons and shall talk of them when you sit in your house and when you walk by the way and when you lie down and when you rise up.
>
> Deuteronomy 6:7

> You [fathers] shall teach them to your sons, talking of them when you sit in your house and when you walk along the road and when you lie down and when you rise up. You shall write them on the doorposts of your house and on your gates, so that your days and the days of your sons may be multiplied on the land which the LORD swore to your fathers to give them, as long as the heavens remain above the earth.
>
> Deuteronomy 11:19–21

> Thorns and snares are in the way of the perverse; he who guards himself will be far from them. Train up a child in the way he should go, even when he is old he will not depart from it.
>
> Proverbs 22:5–6

> Fathers, do not provoke your children to anger, but bring them up in the discipline and instruction of the Lord.
>
> Ephesians 6:4

God's command to be fruitful and multiply and fill the earth shows up in the Bible even before Eve's creation is described (Genesis 1:28). Men have been tasked with this primary role since biblical times. Men are to take seriously this command to generationally transfer kingdom values, not only to their children but also to their grandchildren. God regularly says, "I am the God of Abraham, Isaac, and Jacob," not Sarah, Rebekah, and Rachel, because generational transfer was primarily the responsibility of the father.

This is our responsibility. Yet somehow, a lot of us have forgotten that. The lack of spiritual fruitfulness throughout our land screams this truth. As a result, and as mentioned in the last chapter, Judges 2:10 could easily apply to our world today: "All that generation also were gathered to their fathers; and there arose another generation after them who did not know the LORD." No baton has been passed, leaving only cultural chaos, mayhem, and sheer mess. This summarizes the foundational reason why our country is in the condition it is in. But rather than complain about the situation, let's recognize and acknowledge it and then move on by looking at things we can do to fix it.

And maybe you are not in a situation where you have children to raise. Or perhaps yours are grown. Maybe you never had kids, maybe you're too young to have kids, or maybe you're not married. If any of this applies to you, what I want you to keep in mind is that the legacy you leave behind, whether familial or relational, should be based on these shared biblical principles of transferring kingdom values to the next generation. You *are* leaving a legacy with your life, whether you realize it or not. It may not be a good legacy, but you are making a generational impact through what you do—or don't do. Whether those you influence are your biological seed or not makes little difference in the family of God (see John 19:26–27).

Each of us plays a part in caring for and influencing the next generation. Each of us affects the future. You get to decide if you want to affect it for good by raising up more kingdom men. And keep in mind, no one is too young to do his part. Where I pastor, we started a program called High School Heroes. This program pairs high school students who have demonstrated strong biblical values in their thinking and life choices with younger students at other schools in the district so they can mentor them. This all takes place through the public school system. In fact, we have more than forty schools participating. Men are to impact the next generation in roles as fathers, but we are also to do so outside of fatherhood.

> **Each of us plays a part in caring for and influencing the next generation.**

I'm sure you've seen the word *legacy* attached to sports, athletes, business owners, employees, volunteers, mentors, coaches, friends, and more, because it's all about passing down the DNA of greatness. These principles apply to all of us in the body of Christ too. Thus, the question each of us must address is What kind of legacy are we leaving? And what does Scripture say about how we are to further the futures of those we influence?

Leaving Your Imprint on Humanity

At the beginning of time, God told Adam to fill the earth. Now, he wasn't just tasked with filling it for the sake of filling it. No, Adam was to fill the earth with the image of God. Mankind is made in the image of God. Each of us is to leave our mark on others in human form, to affect people so that the reflection of God and His kingdom values continues to be replicated in history.

God's inheritance never starts with stuff. Not that there is anything wrong with stuff. I'm not speaking against prospering financially or prudently planning to leave a financial inheritance through a will. But what I am saying is if you pass on stuff without the spiritual, it will dissolve in the hands of those you give it to like cotton candy in the mouth of the one who consumes it. Cotton candy might taste sweet for a second, but it has absolutely zero long-term value.

Adam wasn't commissioned to fill the earth with an accumulation of accolades, achievements, and material wealth. He was to fill the earth with the image of God. A divine inheritance isn't about houses, clothes, cars, fame, or money. Divine inheritances start with the transfer of the faith. It doesn't matter how much money a person has if he or she does not have the foundation of a solid faith. Without biblical values, it will all come crashing down when the storms of life roll in. Every kingdom man must be about passing on the spiritual inheritance of a comprehensive theistic world view.

Two predominant grids operate on this earth: humanism and theism. Humanism focuses on mankind and what mankind wants, thinks, and determines. Functioning according to humanism is like putting on sunglasses filtered to reveal the ego's world view. Conversely, theism filters everything through the lens of God's eternal perspective and divine truth.

As kingdom men, we are created and called to transfer a theistic viewpoint to those within our spheres of influence. In this way, we pass on the DNA of the covenant infused in the dominion mandate found in Genesis. We are to pass on the blessing (see Genesis 1:28). The blessing is based on the spiritual.

This concept of passing on the inheritance, or transferring the blessing, is a very big deal in the Bible, as it should be today. We even read one account in which a man manipulated his brother out of his birthright and then conspired with his mom to lie to his father to get his blessing (Genesis 25:29–34; 27:1–17). To better understand the magnitude of the blessing, let's take a closer look at this story.

The Blessing

Jacob was the younger brother of twins born to Rebekah and Isaac. The older brother, Esau, was the athlete. The hunter. His dad's favorite. Jacob, on the other hand, tilled the ground, cooked, and might have even been considered a mama's boy. And since Rebekah loved Jacob so much, she concocted a plan for him to steal the blessing from his older brother.

It happened while Esau was out hunting for the game he needed to bring back to his father for the ceremonial passing of the blessing. When he left, Rebekah instructed Jacob to grab two choice goats so that she could cook them instead. Then, she told her son to dress in some of his brother's clothes. She also put the skins of the goats onto his arms and neck so that her blind, ailing, elderly husband would not be able to easily distinguish him from his brother, who was hairy.

Jacob did as his mom said because the blessing was that important. When his dad asked him how he had gotten the game so quickly, he lied and told him that God had provided it. His dad doubted who he was, so he asked him to come closer so he could feel his hands and face. Confused, Isaac stated, "The voice is the voice of Jacob, but the hands are the hands of Esau" (Genesis 27:22). Then he asked, "Are you really my son Esau?" (v. 24).

"I am" came another of Jacob's lies. Isaac relented and kissed him, smelled his garments one more time, and then blessed him.

I share this story because it illustrates just how critical the blessing truly is. Jacob was willing to conspire with his mom against his dad and brother in order to con, manipulate, and deceive to get it. Why? Because the blessing involves the future. It's so much more than a saying to offer someone after they sneeze or a pat on the back with some positive words. The next two verses in this biblical account shed light on why the blessing is so crucial. We read,

> "Now may God give you of the dew of heaven, and of the fatness of the earth, and an abundance of grain and new wine; may peoples serve you, and nations bow down to you; be master of your brothers, and may your mother's sons bow down to you. Cursed be those who curse you, and blessed be those who bless you."
>
> Genesis 27:28–29

In essence, the blessing involved divine favor. It was the furthering of a great future due to the inheritance of God. It involved God's giving of the dew of heaven, the fatness of the earth, and an abundant supply. Not only that, but it also spoke to how God would respond to the treatment of the person by others. Isaac included curses upon those who would curse Jacob and blessings upon those who would bless him.

Accordingly, at the heart of the transferring of the blessing is the passing on of divine favor, in whatever capacity those in our influence have been gifted to pursue. The blessing is a declaration of divine benefit, divine protection, and divine dominion. This is what we've been called to transfer to the next generation. It's not about giving them a goal or a future role. Let them choose their own goals and roles. Neither is it about giving them stuff. Rather, transferring the blessing is about affirming God's favor and will for their lives.

God Gives the Blessing

It's also essential that we note the specific language of how the blessing began. Isaac started with "May God give. . . ." I highlight this because it seems that this part of the blessing is really missing in our culture today. Far too often, we give a blessing from us, or a dream from us—not from God. Let me explain. We do this by telling those under our care what we want them to do or what we think they can become. Whether to our children or to others we influence, we say things like "I think you could become a doctor," or "Maybe you should be an engineer," or "I think you should play this sport." We even help them along their way.

But the blessing wasn't about helping someone make a name for themselves. It wasn't even about identifying skills. Living in the blessing meant learning to live in divine favor, which then spilled out onto how others both perceived and treated you. It was about doing what God wanted to do in you, for you, and through you.

Just look at the focus we put on transferring or emphasizing other values today, such as athletic success, and it's no wonder we're missing out on transferring the blessing. When a father, uncle, mentor, or friend is never too tired to take someone to practice or cheer each pass, tackle, or home run, but is simply too tired to applaud any amount of spiritual success, we're passing on the wrong values. That's not the blessing.

Truth be told, it doesn't matter how tired some men are—they will find a way to make it to the field for what they feel is important. They'll get there rain or shine. But come Sunday morning? Far too many men are like the abominable snowman on Sunday mornings—their footprints are everywhere, but they are nowhere to be found. We'll be inconvenienced for ball games but not to share the truths of the Bible with those around our own table. That doesn't make any sense at all.

Even so, I'm guilty as well in some of these things. I understand the human pull. When my oldest son, Anthony, was younger, I, like many dads, had a vision for Anthony to play football. I saw his strength, balance, and quickness of hands and knew he should play football. Anthony, on the other hand, didn't share the same vision. Instead of running outside to play football with the neighborhood kids, Anthony would often sit down at the piano. Even as a young child, he did this.

I remember a time when he couldn't have been much older than six or seven and I caught him at the piano. Yes, I used the word *caught* because that's how I viewed it at that time. So I told Anthony to get down from the piano and go outside to play football. He just looked up at me with a confused look on his face. I didn't understand it then like I do now, but I was imposing my own preferences onto him rather than seeking to understand and discover his.

Sure, Anthony looked the part of a football player. He was athletic, fast, and tough. But he didn't have the heart for football. Some of that might have come from the asthma he suffered from as a kid, which could make breathing difficult in a schoolyard game. But it was also due to his interest in animals and music. That's what fascinated him. For the longest time, Anthony wanted to be a veterinarian. And eventually I caught on to the parenting role more so than I did at first, and we were able to encourage him in that regard, as well as in music. Today, as some of you probably know, Anthony is a successful producer, singer, and artist. He even headlined at the Hollywood Bowl as the Beast along with artists such as Kelsey Grammer and Rebel Wilson in *The Beauty and the Beast* orchestra live-to-film.

I'll never forget the time when he was in his late twenties and over at the house having a conversation with me about some of the difficulties he felt growing up in the Evans home. I'm sure other pastors' kids probably face some of these external pressures he spoke about, since so many people closely watch the pastor's family—for a variety of reasons. I didn't agree with or understand everything he was saying, but I could clearly see that he was hurt, which hurt me as well.

Following the conversation, Anthony went back to his room. I knew right then what I needed to do. I went to his room, opened the door, and apologized. I apologized that my son had to feel the things he was feeling and face the pressures he did while growing up, particularly as they related to areas in which I could have done better. I knew that I couldn't go back and change any of it now, but I could apologize to him to promote healing.

Sometimes that's the best we can do. Passing on the blessing isn't always about the pass itself. It's also about clearing the field of any known blockers in the way. You can do this by acknowledging where you dropped the ball and cost one for the team. It's owning your mistakes and letting others know you are sorry that your mistakes or failures negatively affected them. That goes a long way in removing the baggage that could block the transfer of the blessing. If you know of an area where you've let someone down, even if it was in the past, it is still a healing thing to take the time now to let them know you are sorry.

The Authority

Transferring kingdom values involves clearing the way and passing on divine favor, but it can include more. We see this in Numbers 27, where Moses transfers the blessing to Joshua. We are going to look at Moses and Joshua's relationship in greater detail in the next chapter, but I want to highlight the transfer of spiritual authority here. Remember the blessing is spiritual, and even though this specific passage in Numbers doesn't refer to it as a blessing but as a commissioning, Deuteronomy 34:9 (NIV) gives us insight into the spiritual transfer that took place.

> Now Joshua son of Nun was filled with the spirit of wisdom because Moses had laid his hands on him. So the Israelites listened to him and did what the LORD had commanded Moses.

In this passage we read about the spirit of wisdom passed down to Joshua from Moses, which is a transfer of kingdom values and perspective. We also see the divine favor being displayed in how others viewed and treated Joshua as a result of this transfer in that they "listened to him." A blessing can be passed down in many ways and should be passed down to all, but when a person has matured to the point of leading others, it is also important to pass down spiritual authority. We read this in Numbers 27:18–23 (NIV):

> So the LORD said to Moses, "Take Joshua son of Nun, a man in whom is the spirit of leadership, and lay your hand on him. Have him stand before Eleazar the priest and the entire assembly and commission him in their presence. Give him some of your authority so the whole Israelite community will obey him. He is to stand before Eleazar the priest, who will obtain decisions for him by inquiring of the Urim before the LORD. At his command he and the entire community of the Israelites will go out, and at his command they will come in."
>
> Moses did as the LORD commanded him. He took Joshua and had him stand before Eleazar the priest and the whole assembly. Then he laid his hands on him and commissioned him, as the LORD instructed through Moses.

Keep in mind that Joshua hadn't been chosen at random. God told Moses that he had the "spirit of leadership" in him. And as we will see in the next chapter, Joshua had also demonstrated consistent qualities of humility, service, and commitment. God had chosen Joshua to come behind Moses because he would take the mantle and continue the work. No one wants to spend a lifetime building something up only to hand it over to others who are going to mess it up, or to those who don't share the same vision and focus.

The transfer of spiritual authority comes later on in the discipleship process as you recognize those under your influence who have risen to the occasions at hand. You look for those whose lives you have impacted, guided, and transferred biblical values to well. You also look for those to whom God has guided you to transfer spiritual authority. Because Joshua had been a faithful servant, he eventually got his turn to lead.

Far too many men want to lead without serving first. That's backward, Christian soldiers. They want to jump out to the front without learning the fundamentals. Can you imagine what would happen if an NFL coach put in a high school player? The player would get pummeled. I believe that's one reason we are witnessing a large number of Christian leaders retire early or become disqualified from the ministry over scandals or misuse of the power given to them. I believe many had been vested with leadership due to the quick rise of digital platforms without first learning to serve.

Joshua had matured to the point where the blessing of spiritual authority was now his. And because he had spent so much time under the tutelage of Moses, he was able to keep the same vision going, albeit in a different style. He had his own methods, but the core of the ministry remained the same. We see this evidenced in Joshua 8:34–35 (NIV), which says,

> Afterward, Joshua read all the words of the law—the blessings and the curses—just as it is written in the Book of the Law. There was not a word of all that Moses had commanded that Joshua did not read to the whole assembly of Israel, including the women and children, and the foreigners who lived among them.

Joshua faithfully carried out the vision transferred to him by Moses. That's the legacy of generational transfer. That's what the rightful transference of kingdom values, blessings, and authority will produce. It's not a handoff to a different value system. Rather, it's the furthering of the same value system that advances God's kingdom agenda on earth. As a reminder, the kingdom agenda is *the visible manifestation of the comprehensive rule of God over every area of life.*

Transferring the principles of biblical manhood should ultimately lead to future spiritual leadership, as we will look at more fully in the next chapter. When you do it well, the next generation will be positioned to witness their own Jericho walls fall down. They'll get their own victories over Ai. They'll cross their own Jordan rivers. They will topple their own giants with a stone and a slingshot. They will do so because you have given them the tools they need to live out God's kingdom plan for their lives.

In turn, the next generation will then lead others and raise up future kingdom men who do not follow the crowd. They will do this because they will grab the mantle of the blessing, favor, and authority of God.

You Can Ask for the Blessing If You Don't Have It Yet

As we close out this chapter, I want to acknowledge the reality that it's hard to transfer something that was never given to you in the first place. Many men reading these pages never received the blessing themselves. You may never have had a man guide you toward kingdom values. But even if your life has been filled with challenges, difficulties, and spiritual gaps, you can still gain access to the blessing. Divine favor, dominion, and authority are rightfully yours as a child of the King. All you need to do is ask.

That's what Jabez did. And if anyone knew pain, it was Jabez. After all, his mom gave him a name that literally means "pain." Talk about emotional scars being passed down. Every time Jabez heard his name called, he was reminded that he had caused so much pain that his own mom chose to permanently brand him with the label.

> Divine favor, dominion, and authority are rightfully yours as a child of the King.

I don't imagine that your name is Jabez, but I might guess that his name could resemble your soul if this part resonates with you. Perhaps you have no lineage worth revisiting. You have no heritage passed down that is worth honoring. Maybe your mom or your dad resented you as it seems that Jabez's mom resented carrying him. It could be that when you hear other people speaking about families, your heart doesn't fill up with fond memories, but only with ache.

But Jabez didn't let his name define him. Your past doesn't define you either. Jabez didn't let what other people felt about him or said about him become his identity. Like any kingdom man, Jabez desired more. He desired the blessing. So he went directly to the Source.

Now Jabez called on the God of Israel, saying, "Oh that You would bless me indeed and enlarge my border, and that Your hand might be with me, and that You would keep me from harm that it may not pain me!" And God granted him what he requested.

1 Chronicles 4:10

Jabez knew he was made for more than his name. He wasn't satisfied with his station in life. He wasn't content with other people boxing him in as they had. And even if he didn't have anyone to give him the blessing, he was fully aware of the one who could.

Scripture tells us that Jabez was an "honorable" man (1 Chronicles 4:9). It also tells us that those who honor God are honored by God (1 Samuel 2:30). Jabez didn't need a middleman to bless him. He lived an honorable life and, on that basis, went to the Source for more. He got it, as can you.

You may not have had the blessing handed down to you by a father, grandfather, uncle, coach, pastor, leader, or friend. You may feel alone and lost, unable to become all you know you were created to be. But if you choose to honor God through your heart and actions, the transference of kingdom covenantal blessings is yours for the asking. It's never too late to secure your legacy from God.

When I was growing up, one of the things we liked to do was to go bowling. I'd frequently head down to the Lafayette Bowling Alley for a game of duckpin bowling with my friends. It was a pretty rinky-dink bowling alley with short lanes. Most of the time the machines didn't even successfully pick up the pins you'd knocked down. It wasn't unusual to have some pins lying in the lane after your ball had gone through.

To address the situation, management hired someone to walk the lanes and pick up the fallen pins. You'd have to wait a bit as a bowler, but eventually this individual would come to your lane and remove the pins you'd just knocked down.

It was humorous to see the legs and feet of this person running from lane to lane as fast as he could so that the customers could keep bowling. But despite how funny it looked, the system worked. And we all got to bowl our full games.

Things might look funny to you right now. It could be that you've been scrambling around trying to figure life out. Or maybe you've been knocked down so many times that you can no longer get back up on your own, and you need a hand to seize. Whatever the case, God can set things straight again. He can bring people into your life to help you when you need it. He can put you back on your feet again.

God wants you to have the blessing as much as you want to have it. What you've got to do is look to Him, honor Him with your heart and actions, and then ask Him to release the full favor of His blessing and authority on you. Once that's done, you are positioned to transfer the values of the kingdom of God to those within your circle of influence. Each of us can leave a legacy of greatness wherever we are as we rise up as kingdom men.

ELEVEN

IDENTIFYING KEY INFLUENCERS

You can measure the destiny of a team—whether that be a family, workgroup, business, church, community, or even a nation—by its leadership. Unfortunately, today we face a crisis of leadership. People don't know who to follow anymore because this crisis has produced a plethora of poor models and mentors and a complete and utter lack of great leaders.

Yet, God's kingdom program is designed around this process of transferring spiritual wisdom, known as discipleship, in order to produce future leaders. One of the primary roles of kingdom men is to lead others in the way they should go. Another term we often use for leaders is *influencers*. The issue is never whether a man is a leader. As a kingdom man, you are one by nature of your calling. The issue is whether you will be a great leader or a poor one.

That's why I want to look not only at how to be a key influencer, if you aren't already, but also at how to raise up key influencers under your care. In the previous two chapters, we looked at aspects of transferring kingdom values by examining how to live out a successful transfer (Joshua's stones of remembrance), as well as what to transfer (the blessing, favor, and spiritual authority). Now I want us to look at how to identify a potential influencer in the body of Christ and how to make yourself identifiable to those in positions of influence.

The principles apply to both groups of men—whether you are someone of influence looking to mentor and raise up future leaders or you are younger in the faith and want to rise in your calling as a kingdom man. As we come together to mentor and model for each other what true biblical manhood looks like, we are rising up collectively as kingdom men to impact our homes, churches, communities, nation, and world for God and for good.

Raising up a generation of key influencers is never to be done in a top-down way. It happens organically and authentically when men share their lives, experiences, and conversations. Developing key influencers who can solidly speak on biblical truths and navigate the storms of society requires guidance, practice, learning, listening, and so forth. Just like any marriage is dependent on two people contributing for it to be great, identifying and raising up a kingdom influencer requires both men to put forth the effort to learn, grow, listen, teach, discern, practice, model, and more.

The role of coaching gives us great insight into how this takes place. Coaching trees in the NFL help to identify the greatest coaches of all time. A great coach isn't just a man who leads a team to victory. No, a great coach undergirds the futures of all those in his realm of influence. He doesn't own every decision. Rather, he guides and instructs others on how to decide well for themselves.

From Mike Holmgren to Bill Parcells to Marty Schottenheimer, we witness a web of influence that raised up numerous winning coaches such as Tony Dungy, Bill Cowher, Mike McCarthy, Bill Belichick, and others. Legendary coaches leave behind legacies of greatness in other coaches or in the players themselves.[1]

This comes through much more than just Xs and Os. It comes through intentional investment in relationship, listening, learning, and leading. Great leadership knows how to affirm other men, rather than resort to feeling threatened by them. This causes mutual admiration, rather than a feeling of competition between two alpha males.

We saw this played out perfectly in the 2020 Super Bowl win by the Kansas City Chiefs. Players and coaches wanted to win for Coach Reid because they respected him. Through his dedication to them, affection for them, and belief in them, he had earned their loyalty and their desire to give him their greatest effort.

"He's one of the best coaches of all time; he already was before we won this game. But we wanted to get that trophy just because he deserved it. The work that he puts in day in and day out. He's there at like 3 in the morning, and he leaves at 11 [at night]. I don't think he sleeps. I've tried to beat him in, and I never can. He's someone that works harder than anyone I've ever known, and he deserves it."

Patrick Mahomes, MVP of Super Bowl LIV[2]

"We got that ring for Big Red. He acts like a father figure to everyone in the building, and you appreciate that. . . . We're married together forever now."

Travis Kelce, Kansas City Chiefs tight end[3]

"Andy gave me a kiss right on the cheek when we won."

Dave Merritt, Chiefs defensive backs coach[4]

Coaches weren't the only ones getting kisses that Super Bowl–winning day. In fact, when Reid sent Mahomes out for the last play of the game, he did so with unhindered affection. The Kansas City sports columnist reported it this way:

Reid instructed Mahomes to run all the time off the clock and said: "Let's put it down. We've got to use all the time, OK?"
"Yes sir," was Mahomes' response.
Then Reid let out a "ha ha" and gave Mahomes a kiss on the cheek as a father would his son.[5]

Greatness esteems greatness, which leads to even more greatness and influence. One of the most important traits of an influencer is the ability to identify talents in those he influences and draw them out to their highest level. As Andy Reid said of Mahomes shortly before the Super Bowl, "He's got that innate ability to lead. So you give him a little guideline on that, and he takes it and goes."[6] Great leadership knows how to spot great leadership, and then turn it loose within the boundaries of their own guidance.

Choose Well

Nowhere is the principle of choosing well in identifying potential influencers exemplified more clearly than in the relationship between Moses and Joshua. We've touched on the lives of these biblical heroes already, but in this chapter, I want us to examine the components of their relationship that relate to the transference of spiritual influence.

Scripture introduces us to Joshua pretty much out of nowhere in Exodus 17. We have zero background on him. No history. Nothing. All we are told is that he is the son of Nun. He arrives on the scene already in a place of responsibility and recognition. We'll see later in Exodus 24 why he had risen to leadership, but for now, that backstory is kept from the discussion.

Some context for the scene might help explain his abrupt appearance. We read,

> Then all the congregation of the sons of Israel journeyed by stages from the wilderness of Sin, according to the command of the Lord, and camped at Rephidim, and there was no water for the people to drink. Therefore the people quarreled with Moses and said, "Give us water that we may drink." And Moses said to them, "Why do you quarrel with me? Why do you test the Lord?" But the people thirsted there for water; and they grumbled against Moses.
>
> vv. 1–3

This was a difficult group of people facing even more difficult challenges. They had been journeying a long time. Food had become scarce. Water had run dry. Complaining had become the new normal. This crowd feared. It questioned. No doubt they protested and picketed, and if they could have, they would have plastered social media memes mocking their leader, Moses. After all, in their minds he was beyond inept. At best, he lacked planning skills. At worst, he was a tyrant set on his own style of genocide.

Apparently, to them at least, he had led them out of Egypt only to die. Their voices rose against Moses in a rallying cry for their lives, saying, "Why, now, have you brought us up from Egypt, to kill us and our children and our livestock with thirst?" (v. 3). Mob violence threatened to ensue.

We know this by Moses' response: "So Moses cried out to the LORD, saying, 'What shall I do to this people? A little more and they will stone me'" (v. 4). In other words, HELP!

To say that Moses was dealing with a frustrated group of people is an understatement. Moses had been tasked with leading a hungry, thirsty, worn-out, and beleaguered bunch with mutiny on their minds. Moses knew he couldn't do this on his own. That's why he had identified leaders who stood out from the crowd. He had already spotted those who were different. Set apart. Those who established the pace rather than followed it.

Great leadership knows how to spot great leadership.

Joshua didn't follow the complainers. He didn't focus on what he could see. We know this because of how he responded to Moses when Moses sent him into a battle just a few verses later. Joshua set himself to the task at hand, irrespective of the opposition. When Moses told Joshua to command an army for battle despite the lack of supplies, energy, and momentum, Joshua did just that. If he hailed from Texas, he would have said, "Yes, sir." We read,

> Then Amalek came and fought against Israel at Rephidim. So Moses said to Joshua, "Choose men for us and go out, fight against Amalek. Tomorrow I will station myself on the top of the hill with the staff of God in my hand." Joshua did as Moses told him, and fought against Amalek.
>
> Exodus 17:8–10

Joshua didn't shrug his shoulders and remind Moses that his men didn't possess the proper weapons for warfare. Neither did he point out to Moses that just a bit ago it looked as if the people themselves were about to rise up and demand his head. No, when Moses asked Joshua to choose some men and fight against a fierce and well-supplied army, Joshua went. While the crowd focused on what hadn't been done, Joshua focused on what needed to be done.

That's the mark of a kingdom man. Identifying God's hand on a man will have a direct impact on the legacy you leave behind. Who you choose to invest in will reflect back on you. Certain attributes show up in Moses and Joshua's relationship that can give you wisdom on how to identify key influencers and on how to become one yourself.

Attributes of Influencers

Multiple attributes can help you either identify a potential influencer or set yourself up to be identified by others. Every man holds within himself the potential to rise up as a key influencer in his circle. What we need now, more than ever, is a group of kingdom men rising to tackle the challenges our churches and culture face on so many levels. Character qualities and relationship norms such as mutual commitment, a servant spirit, and a great faith will help bring this about.

Mutual Commitment

To exercise your biblical manhood through a position of influence, you need to know where you are headed. You need to have a vision. Visions aren't often birthed in silos. Visions are formulated through studying the lessons of the past and the leaders of the present and combining that with your calling and the calling of those under your care.

A man can do this by listening to those above him and around him. A great mind remains moldable and open to learning from others and following guidance with humility. A great leader constantly works on improving his skills and his game. One way to do this is by studying, listening, and asking questions of those in leadership roles. Kingdom leadership requires both following and leading through a mutual commitment expressed in both men in a relationship, or in the groups of men being poured into.

Moses demonstrated confidence in Joshua to choose the right men and invest in them. Similarly, Joshua demonstrated confidence in Moses' strategy to lead and to win. We know this because it was an unusual strategy at times, to say the least. We read of one such situation in Exodus 17:10–13.

> Moses, Aaron, and Hur went up to the top of the hill. So it came about when Moses held his hand up, that Israel prevailed, and when he let his hand down, Amalek prevailed. But Moses' hands were heavy. Then they took a stone and put it under him, and he sat on it; and Aaron and Hur supported his hands, one on one side and one on the other. Thus his hands were steady until the sun set. So Joshua overwhelmed Amalek and his people with the edge of the sword.

For Joshua to overwhelm and defeat Amalek, he had to believe two things about the man who sent him into battle. First, he had to believe that Moses' staff worked. Secondly, he had to believe that Moses would keep his hands held high. Joshua put his trust in Moses just as Moses had put his trust in Joshua to choose the right men to go to war. Influencing is always a multifaceted, multilayered experience.

Achieving greatness in this life often comes as a result of mutual strengths merged together. Rarely does one man rise to accomplish tremendous things all on his own. There's typically a coach, parent, mentor, pastor, friend, neighbor, teammate, sibling, or teacher—or a combination of those and more—who helps create the context for success. Kingdom men recognize the value of and need for contributors in every aspect of the equation who are committed to a shared overarching goal.

A kingdom leader transfers this value of commitment by demonstrating it and then by identifying and choosing those who value commitment as well.

Unfortunately, commitment has gone missing. We don't see a lot of commitment around. People quit very easily in our culture, especially when things get tough. Over half of all marriages end in divorce. Couples simply give up and quit on each other. Career hopping has become the new normal, with employees quitting after just a year or two to go do something new. It is often linked to the increased pressure that comes with increased responsibilities as jobs develop over time. Just as an employee enters that second or third year when roles get fine-tuned and bigger tasks start to get assigned, tenacity is nowhere to be found. So they start over somewhere else.

A kingdom influencer knows how to remain committed through the tough times as well as through the good. Commitment requires sacrifice, setting your own wants and desires aside, and living with a long-term view of life's meaning and purposes.

Servant Spirit

We gain a glimpse into another attribute of influencers later in Exodus 24 when Moses received the Ten Commandments. Most movies or illustrated Bible storybooks show only Moses on the mountain getting the commandments. Yet if you look closely at the passage, you'll recognize the name of someone who was with him:

> Now the LORD said to Moses, "Come up to Me on the mountain and remain there, and I will give you the stone tablets with the law and the commandment which I have written for their instruction." So Moses arose with Joshua his servant, and Moses went up to the mountain of God. But to the elders he said, "Wait here for us until we return to you."
>
> Exodus 24:12–14

God had told Moses to come up and receive the Ten Commandments. What's more, Joshua went with him. What I want you to notice, first, is how Joshua is defined in the story. It says, "Joshua his servant." This same Joshua who would go on to lead armies, conquests, battles, and a nation wasn't too big to serve. His ego didn't keep him from carrying Moses' bags up a mountainside or helping him in any way necessary. When God called Moses up the mountain, Joshua didn't say, "Hey, I don't want to be number two. I'll sit this one out until it's my turn to shine." No, if he had responded in that way, he would have missed out on this rare event.

After all, the previous verses show us there were a lot of leaders in Israel at that time who could have gone with Moses.

> Then Moses went up with Aaron, Nadab and Abihu, and seventy of the elders of Israel, and they saw the God of Israel; and under His feet there appeared to be a pavement of sapphire, as clear as the sky itself. Yet He did not stretch out His hand against the nobles of the sons of Israel; and they saw God, and they ate and drank.
>
> Exodus 24:9–11

Joshua wasn't the only standout in Israel. Moses had many men who had risen to a place of prominence and influence over the millions who followed them. Yet it was Joshua who was singled out to ascend the mountain for one of the greatest experiences of all time. Sometimes it's not bad being number two. Especially if you get to go with number one up the mountain.

A fundamental rule of biblical manhood is that you don't get to the top without serving first. You don't wake up number one. What's more, a true kingdom man never stops serving.

Unfortunately, today we have a lot of men who want to skip serving and get to the top quick. They want to skip the hard work, dedication, and tenacity required for greatness. I have had young pastors ask me numerous times over the years what the secret is for building a church the size and scope of ours. I know what they mean by the question because there really is no secret at all. They are looking for a secret, but none exists. Common sense tells you it took hard work, grit, commitment, and humility through serving when no one was watching, the lights were out, and no one knew your name. Effort has become a lost quality in our land.

> A fundamental rule of biblical manhood is that you don't get to the top without serving first.

There's no easy way to win a Super Bowl. There's no easy way to win an NBA Championship. Easy ways to write bestsellers or build a successful business don't exist, just like there's no easy way to construct a skyscraper or develop an award-winning film. Anyone who tells you differently is trying to sell you something. It takes hard work to unleash and achieve greatness, no matter what industry you are in. And a good part of that hard work involves your willingness to serve. Jesus put it this way, "But the greatest among you shall be your servant" (Matthew 23:11).

We have far too many men today who want to lead but don't want to follow. They want to lead but refuse to serve. They want to skip straight to number one without any experience at being number two, three, or even ten. But great leaders, great coaches, great men know that you only transfer authority and responsibility to those who have demonstrated the ability to handle it.

You ascend to greatness by descending into a role of service first. No one has ever woken up as the president of a company or a chairman of the board. Key leaders serve their way to the top by performing in a manner that demonstrates the willingness, understanding, character, and responsibility to pull off even greater things.

That is a truism of life itself. Joshua had the privilege of the mountaintop experience because he was willing to serve in the valley. What's more, he was wise enough to serve.

Kingdom men realize that to get somewhere in life, you need to learn from those who have gotten somewhere in life. You need to listen. Take notes. Observe. Ask questions. Contribute. Study. Respect. Acknowledge. And serve. Even if it's boring. Even if it looks like it's going nowhere at all. Joshua modeled this principle of biblical manhood for us. He doesn't broadcast it. Scripture doesn't highlight it. If we're not careful, we might even miss it. I know many have. But right there buried between two tremendous and often-taught-on stories of faith and glory, we get a glimpse of what it means to live as a kingdom man.

It's probably not the verse most pastors preach on. I would imagine it's not even highlighted in your Bible. But I don't want you to miss this, because it holds the DNA for the transference of greatness.

The context tells us that Moses would frequently pitch a tent outside of the camp where he would enter and speak with God (Exodus 33:7–9). I'm sure you've heard the account. People would stand and worship. Then they most likely went about their business while Moses received his instructions from the Lord. All but one person, that is. We read in verse 11 about the dedication and loyalty of Joshua: "When Moses returned to the camp, his servant Joshua, the son of Nun, a young man, would not depart from the tent."

Joshua had determined to do whatever he needed to do to stay close to Moses. Even if that meant hanging outside of a tent for as long as necessary, time and again. That's a leader in the making. Joshua was content to get the crumbs of whatever was falling from the power of God onto Moses in that tent. The residual glory would do. Joshua understood that if he wanted to get close to God, he would need to hang out with someone who already was.

A lot of men are not growing spiritually today because they are not positioning themselves for growth. They are not placing themselves in the proximity of spiritual greatness. You can't run with carnal Christians and expect to rise as a kingdom man. You have to look for men who are already in the right spot. They may not be perfect, but they are close to God. In fact, that's one reason the disciples became such dynamic men. They knew where to hang out. They spent time with Christ. Similarly, Joshua knew where to hang out. He knew how to serve in such a way as to glean, grow, and develop into a great leader.

These qualities and more made Joshua into the legend he became. He combined strength with sensitivity, courage with compassion. He knew how to motivate an army to cross a flooded river or march around an enemy's fortified wall for seven days. But he also knew how to adapt to any situation. He knew when it was time to lead and when it was time to follow. He knew when it was time to talk and when it was time to stand quietly next to a tent for hours and do nothing at all. Serving Moses well helped him learn how to serve God well. Joshua had a heart for God from the start. We see this in how he responded when asked to do reconnaissance in the land with eleven other men. Of all the qualities we've seen in Joshua, this great faith may be the one Moses picked up on first. It's something to look for when identifying potential influencers or making yourself identifiable to others.

Joshua had demonstrated great faith, a servant spirit, and commitment in the midst of confusion and battles fought in unconventional ways. Because of this and more, Joshua rose to become a key leader in the history of Scripture and our world. In light of all that he had overcome, risen to, and accomplished in his own life, Joshua closed out his days with a final charge that reveals this commitment to transferring the faith, which we will explore more fully in the next chapter.

Great Faith

While still young, Joshua stood out from the rest of the leaders in the land. In Numbers 13 we read of the twelve spies being sent to scout out the land so they could give a report of the enemies and what the Israelites would face should they invade. Ten of the men came back shaking in their boots. All they saw were men "of great size" (v. 32). The men's report was so frightening that we read a few verses later, "Then all the congregation lifted up their voices and cried, and the people wept that night" (Numbers 14:1). The report of giants in the land brought the entire nation to their knees in fear.

Except for Joshua and Caleb. Their report was different. They didn't deny the giants. They didn't pretend there were no obstacles or enemies in their way. Rather, they addressed the obstacles. Caleb said, "We should by all means go up and take possession of it, for we will surely overcome it" (Numbers 13:30).

Any man who only sees how big the problem is does not have the spiritual DNA of a kingdom man. I sure don't need men around me telling me how big a problem is. Do you? I can see problems for myself. If there's a giant, he's giant! You don't need to tell me he is a giant. But kingdom men remember who they are. They remember they are giant-slayers. They are Baal fighters. Kingdom men don't run when they face a giant. Instead, they figure out how to maneuver around, go through, climb over, barrel through, or simply out-strategize the opponent.

Bottom line: Kingdom men don't cower when giants tower over them.

The Original Kingdom Man

I'll never forget my dad sitting down with me just a year or so before he passed away. We shared a good conversation as I asked him about how he managed to provide for us so well during seasons of little or no work. He was a longshoreman. Work was seasonal, and money was scarce. Yet we always had food, and we always had our own home. My dad just figured out how to provide for us. Ever positive and continually praising God, my dad rarely complained. I can hardly think of a time that he complained. But he did let one comment slip as we talked that day.

"How'd you do it, Dad?" I asked, "Didn't you want to quit when it got hard?"

"No," he replied with a firmness reflective of the strength of his will.

"What kept you going then?" I pushed to know more.

"Well, Tony," he said, "knowing the Lord and obeying what He would have me to do because He bought me with a price. And that price is God's Son the Lord Jesus Christ when He said it was finished on the cross."

He makes it sound so easy, doesn't he? But it wasn't. My dad continued, "Times got so tough that I had to rent part of our house out just to try to keep it and pay the mortgage. I worked two or three jobs doing whatever

I could. I was under tremendous pressure in those days. I had migraine headaches as well, which came from a lot of this great pressure on me to provide for all of you."

I had never heard my dad talk of his headaches before. Like I said, he didn't complain. He always pointed out the things he was grateful for. But somehow knowing the pressure he faced was also coupled with physical pain created by stress made what he sacrificed and accomplished for us all the more noble. Kingdom men don't throw in the towel because things get hard. I've seen that firsthand.

David was another kingdom man who didn't cower in front of a giant. That's one reason God chose him to eventually become king. Saul and the armies of Israel looked on Goliath and trembled. David saw the giant and strategized a plan for his defeat. Kingdom men don't run away in the face of adversity. They don't bail. Chumps run. Chumps bail. Kingdom men rise up because when everyone else is chanting, "We can't," there's one voice that quietly, yet firmly, responds, "Why not?"

Scripture has already made it clear that we can do all things through Christ who strengthens us (Philippians 4:13). That's the criterion you are to base your decisions on. Is God leading you into battle? Is God asking you to speak up at work? Has God placed a problem in your path that He wants you to influence and sort out for others' good and His glory? If God has given the challenge to you or allowed it into your life, then you are man enough to face it head on and overcome.

I understand that you may have had a difficult upbringing. I am not denying that there are inequities and disparities still at play in our culture. I'm fully aware that broken systems contribute to broken structures, which can lead to broken lives. But it's not about the giant standing in front of you. It's about what you hold in your hand. What experience, awareness, skill, or tool has God given you to overcome the opposition?

> What experience, awareness, skill, or tool has God given you to overcome the opposition?

Whatever it is, you'd better use it. I've been around long enough to know that despite all the talk and well-wishes and seminars, systems rarely change completely. Embedded structures are often difficult to improve holistically, and prejudices often remain—whether it is prejudice against a particular race, culture, class, or background. It doesn't matter the details; what matters is what's in your hand.

If a shepherd boy can slay a giant with a stone, there is no telling what God can do through you and through me.

I was the fourth black student admitted to Dallas Theological Seminary. The fourth one. I've known my share of obstacles. I've had my share of looks, attitudes, and dismissals. I didn't cower and cry beneath a reality that made it very clear I had to be three times better just to get the same acknowledgment. I didn't whine when someone made a racist statement or tried to block me from moving ahead. Every time I came across one of those guys with those attitudes, I chose to rise above it. I chose to let it motivate me rather than defeat me. What other people do or say has no bearing on how you respond.

As a result, my work ethic grew stronger. Eventually, I became the first African American to earn a doctorate degree at Dallas Theological Seminary and the first to write a full study Bible and Bible commentary. I didn't realize that would be the case when I decided to go on the ten-year journey of studying and writing about the parts of Scripture I hadn't yet preached on in the previous forty years of ministry. I just saw the concept as a great thing to do—explore God's Word, learn for myself, and expand my preaching while also giving people a holistic kingdom view of Scripture.

But as I neared the completion of the commentary, talk started surrounding the release about how I was the first African American to write one. *That's great*, I thought. In fact, the Museum of the Bible created a display for the commentary as a historical piece. You can see it when you visit the Museum in Washington, DC.

But I began to wonder, if I was the first African American to write a full study Bible and Bible commentary, how many people overall had written one? So I reached out to my publisher to see if they could find out. They did some research and relayed back to me that most commentaries are typically comprised of work from several authors or theologians. And while some people had written commentaries on specific books of the Bible, only one other living author had a full-Bible commentary published entirely in his name. I knew the commentary had been a lot of work, commitment, and tiresome early mornings and late nights. But I hadn't realized that, most likely because of those challenges, few had ever done it.

Adversity and challenges have a way, if you let them, of sharpening your skills, strengthening your will, and focusing your approach to your goals and dreams. They can cause you to rise higher than people ever expected you to go, or higher than you thought you would go. But it all depends on how you choose to view and respond to the difficulties that come your way. Will you respond in great faith, or will you respond in blame, bitterness, or fear? It's your choice. But whatever choice you make will also determine the outcome you, and generations after you, face.

I'll always remember the trip I took to DC to see my commentary on display at the Museum of the Bible. I went with Priscilla and her family as well as with Anthony. Walking up to the display case to witness my very own work beneath the glass, along with a note detailing why it was chosen for display, was overwhelming. If you saw any of the video footage that Priscilla and Anthony captured on their phones that day, you heard my awe and saw me mouth the words "This is weird."

It can be a little weird to see something you've worked on put in a museum. Historical museum displays typically happen after a person has transitioned to glory. But God gave me both the honor and joy of experiencing this on earth.

The weekend was a roller coaster of emotion, though, due to the other reason I had taken the trip. One reason, of course, was to see the commentary on display. This produced a very high level of emotion and satisfaction. The other reason, though, was to travel to Baltimore to handle some housing and paper work items for my father, the original kingdom man, as he had passed away not two weeks earlier. This, obviously, produced emotion due to the pain and loss.

Yet as I went through some of his papers and walked once more through the house he and my mom had raised us in, it struck me how proud he would have been to see his son's Bible commentary on permanent display at a prestigious museum in DC. I'm sure he would have kidded me about it at first, as he always did. And he definitely would have reminded me not to get the big head. But deep down, I know he would have been proud.

After all, the Bible commentary in the museum is not just my legacy. It is also his. My dad committed to following Christ as a young father of four, and as a result, many in his family have also gone on to live under the lordship of Jesus Christ. As for Arthur Evans and his house, he chose to serve the Lord. For that, I will be forever grateful.

TWELVE

STARTING THE TRANSFER

King me.

You've heard the phrase. A person says it when playing checkers and their piece reaches the last row on their opponent's side of the board. Maybe you've said it yourself. It means you get to elevate your piece to the rank of king. This brings with it the ability to move in a diverse set of directions.

While I'm sure you have heard the phrase "king me," you probably have not heard of the man who has said it more times than anyone else—ever. His name was Marion Tinsley. Born in 1927, he was the son of a farmer and a schoolteacher. Tinsley made his mark in academics early on, graduating high school at the age of fifteen. He quickly went on to soar through college and later earn a doctorate in the mathematical discipline of combinatorial analysis.

Marion's reign as checkers champion surpasses any athlete, mental or physical, in sheer dominance and length of time. A nine-time World Champion, he went undefeated in all matches for forty years. For four decades, no one even came close to besting him. He was a legend. In fact, it was said that he had a "better-than-computer-like-grasp" on how to play and could predict thirty moves ahead.[1] The second-best player of all time once offered this praise: "Marion Tinsley is to checkers what Leonardo da Vinci was to science, what Michelangelo was to art and what Beethoven was to music."[2]

Now, for those of you who think checkers is just a game you play on Saturday with your kids, think again. While the rules of the game may be simple, the strategy is anything but. There are 500 billion billion different board positions.[3] Yes, you read that right. It's 500 billion *billion*. Checkers champions don't become champions by luck. In fact, it is said that Tinsley once stated he spent more than 10,000 hours studying checkers in graduate school alone.[4] Perhaps Tinsley is the actual impetus of Malcolm Gladwell's 10,000-hour rule theory he writes about in *Outliers: The Story of Success*. Tinsley innately knew that succeeding required study as well as practice. In fact, he chose not to marry; he once said he'd never seen a checker marriage that worked out.

What he did do for social engagement and service to humanity, though, was assist as a lay minister in a predominantly black church in Tallahassee, Florida. He also taught math at the historically black Florida Agricultural and Mechanical University (FAMU) for twenty-six years. Tinsley was white. He had left Florida State University to teach at FAMU during the late 1960s, a time of heightened racial unrest. A yearbook during his tenure reveals he was probably the only white person over age forty on the campus.[5]

He had considered moving to Africa to become a missionary, but he was sharply rebuked by a friend, he told *Sports Illustrated*. "I had thought of going to Africa as a self-supporting missionary until a sharp-tongued sister pointed out to me that most people who wanted to help blacks in Africa wouldn't even talk to blacks in America."[6]

Obviously, Tinsley based his life choices on his convictions to make the world a better place. This investment did not go unnoticed. In his obituary, one of his former colleagues had this to say: "At his retirement dinner, literally everybody; young, old, black, white, students, faculty members . . . gave testimonies about the impact he had had on their lives."[7]

No doubt Tinsley also based his choices in checkers on this same level of confident commitment and belief. We can assume this because of his willingness to agree to a battle for the championship against something, not someone, that many unwaveringly believed would beat him. By 1992 a highly designed artificial intelligence program, Chinook, had appeared on the scene. By then, this AI could see options so far into the future that lead programmer Jonathan Schaeffer was certain no human could beat it. Nearly all in the checkers community felt the same.

All except for Tinsley. When asked if he was concerned about AI beating him, he responded calmly, "I have a better programmer than Chinook. His was Jonathan, mine was the Lord."[8]

The first nine games of the match proved to be incredibly challenging, each ending in a draw. In the tenth game, however, the AI made a costly move, despite having the ability to search an extreme number of probabilities far into the future. When Tinsley saw the move, he declared, "You're gonna regret that."[9]

The computer programmer discarded Tinsley's statement as nothing more than bravado. Of course his AI would win, or so he assumed. He had thought it could predict beyond humanity's proven ability to do so. But Jonathan was wrong. From that point forward, Tinsley pulled ahead in the game and ultimately won. According to Schaeffer, in Tinsley's notes on the game summarizing the win, Tinsley penned that he had seen all of the moves from that point in the game clear to the end. He knew he had the victory right then.[10]

Well into his sixties by that time, Tinsley lived out the remainder of his days as champion over both man and machine. When he died, fittingly in Humble, Texas, a humble man despite all of his achievements, his modest tombstone had a checkerboard in the upper right corner. In the upper left was "Let brotherly love continue," a reference to Hebrews 13:1.

Tinsley's assurance of God's favor and wisdom in his life enabled him to rise to heights of greatness rarely achieved by any. He attributed his success to God, as he once told the *Chicago Tribune*.

> "Out of the clear blue sky an improvement of a published play will just come to mind, as if the subconscious has been working to come to light. A lot of my discoveries come that way, out of the clear blue sky. Some of my insights into the Scriptures come the same way."[11]

Tinsley's life could easily be described as one of the greatest in modeling the truths of biblical manhood in modern times. In many ways, he consistently demonstrated that

God is the Source of all wisdom and gives it freely (James 1:5).

God desires for us to live in unity (John 13:35).

God knows the end from the beginning (Isaiah 46:10).

Even AI must bow to the one, true King (Ephesians 4:6).

The man who said "king me" more than any other man who ever lived was truly a kingdom man at heart. He did what kingdom men do. Kingdom men live a life that both models and guides others on how to live according to spiritual principles of manhood. Many men would have cowered beneath an opponent the world predicted to win. Why not hang on to the undefeated status a bit longer by picking and choosing who you play?

Why not? Because that's not what kingdom men do. Kingdom men rise to overcome the obstacles at hand—they don't run from them.

Similarly, many men would have remained in their culturally singular environments, teaching at well-paying universities. Why intentionally enter the fray of racial unknowing?

Why? Because that's what kingdom men do. They rise to the occasion before them, and in so doing, raise the bar.

As kingdom men, we are to do no less. We are to rise above the obstacles looming large before us in our land. We must never back down or run away. Instead, we are to set a new standard. Establish a new pace. Boldly declare that we, as men, no longer accept the evil nor the divisions that the culture demands remain. We must do this for ourselves, but we also must do this with, and for, each other. *Kingdom Men Rising* isn't about living as a lone ranger Christian. It's a call for men to collectively respond to the need for a fresh troop of kingdom warriors to take their stand.

Do Not Choose Poorly[12]

As I wrote in *Raising Kingdom Kids*, I love the Indiana Jones movies. I love the adventure, chase, intrigue, and ultimate conquests that show up in each one. Indiana Jones overcame every obstacle and scaled every wall in order to claim the prize. But victory didn't always come simply through brawn and resolve; most often it required wise maneuvering as well.

One of my all-time favorite scenes is when Jones is chasing after the elusive Holy Grail in *Indiana Jones and the Last Crusade*. Maybe you remember this scene as well. Through many dangers, toils, and snares, Indiana Jones makes it safely to his final challenge—one that would test his wisdom. In this scene, Indiana Jones is standing in the candle-lit grail sanctuary in the Temple of the Sun, guarded continuously by the aged, yet ageless, Grail Knight.

In the room are dozens of chalices and bowls, each with a unique style and imprint. The final test to prove one's worthiness to obtain the true treasured cup is to search through the various chalices and choose the one true grail.

The revelation of whether that choice was correct would come when the person took their chosen cup, filled it from the font of the chamber, and sipped. If they had chosen the Holy Grail, they would live. If they had chosen any other chalice, they would quickly experience a painful death.

As Indiana Jones and the other characters in the film first enter the grail sanctuary, they are met by the Grail Knight, who explains what they are to do, and then adds these words of warning: "Choose wisely," he says, pausing to let it sink in, "for as the true grail will bring you life, the false grail will take it from you."[13]

The antagonist chooses first. He chooses poorly. As a result, he dies and decomposes right there in front of everyone's eyes. Indiana Jones's turn is next. He looks around and around, confused because they all look right. They all seem like they could be the one. But then, all of a sudden, he notices something.

Off to the side sits a small wooden chalice. Just one, in the midst of all the glittery and shiny and larger ones. This wooden one catches his attention because he remembers that Jesus was a carpenter. Jesus dealt with wood. He wasn't into all the fancy extras the other cups display. So Indiana Jones goes over and picks the wooden one. He chooses wisely. As a result, both he and his ailing father live.

True, the Indiana Jones films are just films for entertainment. But this scene echoes with the profound reality nestled in God's Word. God has given each of us a choice. Deuteronomy 30:19 puts it this way:

I call heaven and earth to witness against you today, that I have set before you life and death, the blessing and the curse. So choose life in order that you may live, you and your descendants.

As we have seen throughout our time together, we choose life by basing our decisions on the wisdom of God's Word. His commandments, precepts, and principles exist to show us how we are to live a life comprised of wisdom. As you make your choices today, there are a lot of shimmery options out there. They may seem right. They may look enticing. But the real question is whether your choice is one that Jesus himself would authorize. Because if it's not what Jesus would authorize—or a cup from which He would drink—all you will experience is disintegration and ultimate death. More failure. More frustration. More loss.

Yet if you choose wisely, the truth of God's Word will bring life, not only to you but also to those around you.

When you apply God's wisdom to your life by living in accordance with what He has outlined in Scripture, you are setting yourself up for spiritual success. Wisdom is the way to experience God's will and His favor, because wisdom is the application of God's will to the practical areas of life.

> **Cultural change starts with one man making one wise choice.**

We are living in a day when the proverbial fork in the road is more pronounced than ever. When you examine all that is happening around us—the chaos, confusion, lack of clarity, and voices coming at us from all directions—it is clear that it is time for men to make a choice. Will you choose wisely and live? Or will you choose poorly? Cultural change starts with one man making one wise choice. And it starts right now.

Living Out Your Kingdom Declaration

The choice is yours. But while the choice is yours, I want to remind you that you don't get to choose the consequences. All consequences are in the hand of God. Isaiah chapter 3 makes it clear what happens when men do not choose well. The younger generation wind up in rebellion, oppression ensues, and chaos reigns. We read,

> For behold, the Lord GOD of hosts is going to remove from
>   Jerusalem and Judah . . .
> The mighty man and the warrior. . . .
> And I will make mere lads their princes,
> And capricious children will rule over them,
> And the people will be oppressed,
> Each one by another, and each one by his neighbor;
> The youth will storm against the elder
> And the inferior against the honorable. . . .
> For Jerusalem has stumbled and Judah has fallen,
> Because their speech and their actions are against the LORD,
> To rebel against His glorious presence. . . .
> And they display their sin like Sodom;
> They do not even conceal it.
> Woe to them!
> For they have brought evil on themselves. . . .
> Woe to the wicked! It will go badly with him,
> For what he deserves will be done to him.
> O My people! Their oppressors are children,
> And women rule over them.
> O My people! Those who guide you lead you astray
> And confuse the direction of your paths.
>
> Isaiah 3:1–2, 4–5, 8–9, 11–12

As a result of abdicating their biblical kingdom roles, the men became weak and fell by the sword (v. 25). Unfortunately, this all sounds very similar to the day and age in which we live. Too many men are operating outside of their divinely ordained responsibilities, thus causing all of us to fall by the sword of societal unrest. What we need are men who are willing to not only declare, as Joshua did in Joshua 24, that they are kingdom men, but also live like they are.

Joshua also led a nation in the midst of countless voices seeking to "confuse the direction" of their paths. That's why he challenged his men by declaring his stand for God. He declared that his decisions would not be defined by the cultural norms around him. His commitment was to the will and Word of God, not to the world. Joshua knew that the pressure of society as well as the environment of the Amorites would lead to a propensity toward spiritual compromise, so he asked the men of his land to make a declaration similar to his (Joshua 24:14–28).

We read the primary statements in Joshua's final charge in verses 14–15:

> "Now, therefore, fear the LORD and serve Him in sincerity and truth; and put away the gods which your fathers served beyond the River and in Egypt, and serve the LORD. If it is disagreeable in your sight to serve the LORD, choose for yourselves today whom you will serve: whether the gods which your fathers served which were beyond the River, or the gods of the Amorites in whose land you are living; but as for me and my house, we will serve the LORD."

This takes us back to the beginning, where we started with a call to serve God and influence others to do the same. Joshua reminded the men of Israel to fear God. He charged them to take God seriously. This mind-set would then play out in how they served Him and influenced their culture for God and for good. They were not to chase after money, power, platforms, or pleasure like those who worshiped the gods and idols of that day. Rather, they were to worship the one true God who rules over all.

Following Joshua's charge to the men of Israel, he let them know where he stood as well. "As for me and my house, we will serve the LORD," he said, in that now famous line. Joshua showed no hesitation in speaking for his whole family, because he spoke as a kingdom man. On his deathbed, he reinforced his declaration for his home. The Israelite men responded that they would take down the idols and serve God too, after which Joshua established a covenant with them. We read,

> The people said to Joshua, "We will serve the LORD our God and we will obey His voice." So Joshua made a covenant with the people that day, and made for them a statute and an ordinance in Shechem. And Joshua wrote these words in the book of the law of God; and he took a large stone and set it up there under the oak that was by the sanctuary of the LORD. Joshua said to all the people, "Behold, this stone shall be for a witness against us, for it has heard all the words of the LORD which He spoke to us; thus it

shall be for a witness against you, so that you do not deny your God." Then Joshua dismissed the people, each to his inheritance.

It came about after these things that Joshua the son of Nun, the servant of the LORD, died, being one hundred and ten years old. And they buried him in the territory of his inheritance in Timnath-serah, which is in the hill country of Ephraim, on the north of Mount Gaash. Israel served the LORD all the days of Joshua and all the days of the elders who survived Joshua, and had known all the deeds of the LORD which He had done for Israel.

vv. 24–31

That's an interesting epitaph on Joshua's tombstone. The only thing we read of him, essentially, is that he is "the servant of the LORD." The bottom line: Joshua served the purposes of God while on earth. As a result, we discover that Israel also "served the LORD all the days of Joshua." The transfer took root and bore fruit. What's more, Joshua's legacy equipped and inspired them to serve God "all the days of the elders who survived Joshua" as well. That's what generational transfer looks like, men. That's what it means to live and to lead as a kingdom man.

As we saw in the previous chapter, Joshua started his ministry with qualities such as commitment, servanthood, and a great faith. He wasn't too proud to stand outside the tent of meeting for hours on end. He hadn't thought too highly of himself to carry supplies up a mountain. He didn't balk when battle strategies seemed odd, nor did he retire when he reached a certain age. No, Joshua's departing declaration to his nation came at the age of one hundred ten. As a result, Joshua left a legacy of life, peace, and greatness not only to his own family but to his entire nation.

A kingdom man should do no less.

As we come to the close of our time together in this book, I want you to consider the legacy you are leaving behind.

Is it a legacy that inspires spiritual excellence in others?

Have you made your declaration loud and clear?

Will you rise, and join with other kingdom men who are also rising, to leave a mark of greatness as we advance God's kingdom agenda on earth?

If you answered *yes*, then take a moment to add your own personal declarations in the Kingdom Declaration that I have for you in appendix A. Then sign it. Writing it down reinforces the declaration in your spirit, mind, and soul. I encourage you to do it, even if you leave it in the book after you're done.

It is only when men stand up, stand strong, and declare what is right and true that the influence of positive impact will be felt. Joshua's Kingdom Declaration did not deny the reality of the day nor the humanity of each man, but it did state that these things were to be subject to a higher authority and greater good. To sum it up, he declared that he would put God first.

What you and I must never forget is that God has an exclusivity clause. He cannot be second. My great concern with all of the cultural turmoil we are going through is that while we may be calling on God and praying to God, we also have competing idols consuming our attention. These so-called American idols are sophisticated. Subtle. An idol might be technology. It could be politics. Celebrities. Sports. Status. It might even be one's race, income, entertainment, or career. As I've stated before, anything that overrules God in your decision-making—including another relationship—is an idol.

When you exalt an idol over God, you have removed Him from the equation. This is because God will excuse himself from participating or intervening, even though you may be praying to Him for help.

Far too many men want a cafeteria god. This is the kind of god that you pick and choose when you want him and when you don't want him. That's not the kind of God He is, and that's not the kind of man He is looking to partner with in impacting the world. God doesn't want you just voting for Him in private. He is not seeking a silent majority. God calls each of us to publicly declare our allegiance to Him above all else. It is then that He will join us to address the issues at hand.

And we have some rather big issues at hand right now, if you haven't noticed. I'm sure you have. We have all kinds of pandemics in our land. From health pandemics to racial pandemics to police and community pandemics to political and economic pandemics—we are facing clashes everywhere. The resolution to these pandemics, and more, is kingdom men taking their stand and speaking out while also modeling what God says about each area.

We are to display and teach what God says about racial injustice.
We are to reflect and explain what God says about law and order.
We are to show and inform on what God says about healing past traumas and wounds.
We are to reveal and state what God says about how we are to relate to each other, speak to each other, and invest in each other.

God has something to say on every subject in front of us, and He has not stuttered. If we are going to make a difference of healing, oneness, justice, and righteousness in a broken world, we must get our own lives together first and then come together in a like-minded approach to impacting the culture. Yes, the past may house its mistakes. But we can start right now to make a better tomorrow.

The Challenge at Hand

The time is now to start investing in a biblical generational transfer. A lesson of letting go of the past and starting now to make a better future revealed itself fully in a great friend's life not too long ago. I met Sherman Smith and his wife when he was just a young player for the Seahawks and I was a speaker at the Pro Athletes Outreach annual conference decades ago. They quickly became family friends. Over the years, Sherman even coached my son Jonathan when he was a Tennessee Titan and a Washington Redskin.

Sherman later went on to serve as the running backs coach for the Seahawks for seven of his thirty-three coaching years. I celebrated with him when they grabbed their Super Bowl win. I also sorrowed with him when the Hawks opted for a pass over sending Beast Mode (Marshawn Lynch) up the middle from the one-yard line to secure their second Super Bowl win. I think the whole country sorrowed with him—everyone outside of Boston that is! Many in Seattle still do.

Sherman handled the loss well and with maturity. But that didn't surprise me. He had always struck me as a man of character, dedication, and great Christian faith. But how he handled the news he received a few years ago amazed me all the more.

You may have seen his story on the ESPN *30 for 30* show. Or perhaps you read his story online. I encourage you to look it up and watch the show. It is inspiring. But the short of it is that unbeknown to him, Sherman fathered a child just before heading off to college, yet had never been told.

His son had been put up for adoption by the young lady Sherman had been intimate with at that time. She moved to Pittsburgh to give birth so that no one would know. Yet now, some forty years later, Sherman got a call from a man he knew very well. A man he already loved like a son. A man he had scouted in college, recruited, and coached himself. A man who others had said over the years looked like he could be his son. A man he had actively mentored and who admired him as the father figure in his life. Sherman had watched this man go on to perform outstandingly in college, and he wound up coaching running backs in the NFL, just as Sherman did. In fact, he coached running backs for a Super Bowl winning team too, the Kansas City Chiefs.

Sounds similar to "like father, like son."

That's because it is.

They just didn't know it.

The man's name was Deland McCullough. He had been adopted as a baby. Four decades later, as an adult, he set out to locate his birth mom and dad. What he discovered was life changing. The man he had looked up to most, his coach, friend, and mentor, Sherman Smith, was in fact his biological father.

After a time of initial shock and DNA testing to be sure, Sherman reveled in the reality that this young man he loved was his son. Yet even in the joy, he told me he struggled with the guilt. Knowing that he had not been there for his son during his developmental years broke his heart. A loving, dedicated family man, this failure on his part—even though he had no way of knowing at the time—ate him up inside. The grief and guilt sought to steal the opportunity for influencing and investing in the present.

It wasn't until Sherman made the decision to let go of the past and forgive himself that he was able to embrace the now. He leaned across the table as he shared this story with us over dinner, as if to emphasize this powerful truth: "I knew I couldn't undo the past or my failures, but I also knew I could start right now to build a relationship with him and his family, my grandsons, from this moment forward. I had a choice to make: Stay stuck in the past. Or start new."

That's wisdom. That's a kingdom man kind of move.

Men, while you cannot go back and correct mistakes or redeem passed time, it's up to you to determine how things will go from here on out. It's all about the choices you make right now. Let go of the past. It only exists to inform your present, not to hold you back from a better tomorrow. Your future depends on the decisions you make right now.

This reminds me of the story of two college men who wanted to trick their professor. This professor was known for being very smart and always having an answer for every question. So these two men set out to see if they could stump him. They decided to catch a bird and bring it to him in one of their hands.

Walking up to the professor, one of the young men said, "Professor, I am holding a bird in my hand. Is it dead or alive?" The two men knew that if the professor said the bird was alive, they could squeeze it so that it was no longer alive. If the professor said the bird was dead, all they needed to do was release it and let it fly away. Either way, they assumed they would prove the professor wrong.

But this was a very wise professor, so when he was confronted with the question, he answered quickly. Glancing at the hand holding the bird, and then looking back up at the young men, he answered, "Gentlemen, you asked me a question—is the bird dead or alive. The answer to the question is in your hand. It is what you decide."

We face a culture that wants to trick us, trip us up, and get us to make the wrong decisions or give the wrong replies. But the answer to whether we will experience life or death in our walk as men is actually in our own hands. Satan only looks to be winning this war on the world because kingdom men have illegitimately handed him the ball. It's not because Satan is more powerful. He's not. Our futures, and the futures of our families, churches, communities, and nation, are in our own hands. They are based on what we decide.

> If we, as kingdom men, collectively choose to follow Christ by cultivating a relationship with Him and submitting to His rule, we will produce life.

If we, as kingdom men, collectively choose to follow Christ by cultivating a relationship with Him and submitting to His rule, we will produce life. Any other path we pursue will result in further destruction. The choice is ours to make. The time to make that choice is now.

Men, it is high time we rise up as one voice and one example for each other, our families, our churches, our communities, and our land. It's time we take our positions on the field. Grab what you've got. Use it. Make your moves. Sure, your opponents may be tall, strong, or even programmed to beat you. But you know the one who knows the end from the beginning. The one who crafted and created you has already determined His purposes will be carried out. As it is written,

"Declaring the end from the beginning, and from ancient times things which have not been done, saying, 'My purpose will be established, and I will accomplish all My good pleasure.'"

Isaiah 46:10

God will do it. The victory is already His. It's your role to walk in His established purpose for your life. It's your responsibility to intentionally and strategically progress forward. It's your time to barrel past the opposition and boldly declare, "King me." Then, lead the way for others to do the same.

It's your move.

APPENDIX A

KINGDOM DECLARATION

1. Whereas God created the man to be primarily responsible for advancing His kingdom agenda.

2. Whereas God has positioned men as heads of their families.

3. Whereas God holds men accountable and responsible for maintaining an intimate relationship with Him.

4. Whereas God requires men to love and lead their wives.

5. Whereas God has given men the primary responsibility for raising their children.

6. Whereas God has determined for men to oversee the spiritual leadership and direction of the church.

7. Whereas God holds men accountable for the spiritual condition of the culture.

8. Whereas God will hold men accountable at the judgment seat of Christ for how they fulfilled their divinely assigned role and responsibility.

I, _____, declare today that I commit the remainder of my life to fulfilling my created calling to function as a kingdom disciple in my walk with God, leadership of my family, commitment to my church, and influencing of my community.

Signature _____

Date_____

APPENDIX B

THE URBAN ALTERNATIVE

The Urban Alternative (TUA) equips, empowers, and unites Christians to impact *individuals, families, churches,* and *communities* through a thoroughly kingdom agenda world view. In teaching truth, we seek to transform lives.

The core cause of the problems we face in our personal lives, homes, churches, and societies is a spiritual one; therefore, the only way to address it is spiritually. We've tried political, social, economic, and even religious agendas.

It's time for a **kingdom agenda**.

> *The kingdom agenda can be defined as the visible manifestation of the comprehensive rule of God over every area of life.*

The unifying central theme throughout the Bible is the glory of God and the advancement of His kingdom. The conjoining thread from Genesis to Revelation—from beginning to end—is focused on one thing: God's glory through advancing God's kingdom.

When you do not recognize that theme, the Bible becomes disconnected stories that are great for inspiration but seem to be unrelated in purpose and direction. Understanding the role of the kingdom in

Scripture increases the relevancy of this several-thousand-year-old text to your day-to-day living, because the kingdom is not only then; it is now.

The absence of the kingdom's influence in our personal lives, family lives, churches, and communities has led to a deterioration in our world of immense proportions:

- People live segmented, compartmentalized lives because they lack God's kingdom world view.
- Families disintegrate because they exist for their own satisfaction rather than for the kingdom.
- Churches are limited in the scope of their impact because they fail to comprehend that the goal of the church is not the church itself, but the kingdom.
- Communities have nowhere to turn to find real solutions for real people who have real problems because the church has become divided, ingrown, and unable to transform the cultural and political landscape in any relevant way.

The kingdom agenda offers us a way to see and live life with a solid hope by optimizing the solutions of heaven. When God is no longer the final and authoritative standard under which all else falls, order and hope leave with Him. But the reverse of that is true as well: As long as you have God, you have hope. If God is still in the picture, and as long as His agenda is still on the table, it's not over.

Even if relationships collapse, God will sustain you. Even if finances dwindle, God will keep you. Even if dreams die, God will revive you. As long as God and His rule are still the overarching standard in your life, family, church, and community, there is always hope.

Our world needs the King's agenda. Our churches need the King's agenda. Our families need the King's agenda.

We've put together a three-part plan to direct us in healing the divisions and striving for unity as we move toward the goal of truly being one nation under God. This three-part plan calls us to assemble with others in unity, address the issues that divide us, and act together for social impact.

Following this plan, we will see individuals, families, churches, and communities transformed as we follow God's kingdom agenda in every area of our lives. You can request this plan by emailing info@tonyevans.org, or you can find it online at tonyevans.org.

In many major cities, there is a loop that drivers can take when they want to get somewhere on the other side of the city but don't necessarily want to head straight through downtown. This loop will take you close enough to the city so that you can see its towering buildings and skyline, but not close enough to actually experience it.

This is precisely what we, as a culture, have done with God. We have put Him on the "loop" of our personal, family, church, and community lives. He's close enough to be at hand should we need Him in an emergency, but far enough away that He can't be the center of who we are.

We want God on the loop, not the King of the Bible who comes downtown into the very heart of our ways. Leaving God on the loop brings about dire consequences as we have seen in our own lives and with others. But when we make God, and His rule, the centerpiece of all we think, do, and say, it is then that we will experience Him in the way He longs for us to experience Him.

He wants us to be kingdom people with kingdom minds set on fulfilling His kingdom's purposes. He wants us to pray, as Jesus did, "Not my will, but Thy will be done." Because His is the kingdom, the power, and the glory.

There is only one God, and we are not Him. As King and Creator, God calls the shots. It is only when we align ourselves underneath His comprehensive hand that we will access His full power and authority in all spheres of life: personal, familial, ecclesiastical, and governmental.

As we learn how to govern ourselves under God, we then transform the institutions of family, church, and society using a biblically based kingdom world view.

Under Him, we touch heaven and change earth.

To achieve our goal, we use a variety of strategies, approaches, and resources for reaching and equipping as many people as possible.

Broadcast Media

Millions of individuals experience *The Alternative with Dr. Tony Evans* through the daily radio broadcast playing on nearly **1,400 radio outlets** and in over **130 countries**. The broadcast can also be seen on several television networks and is available online at tonyevans.org. You can also listen or view the daily broadcast by downloading the Tony Evans app for free in the App store. Over 30 million message downloads or streams occur each year.

Leadership Training

The Tony Evans Training Center (TETC) facilitates a comprehensive discipleship platform that embodies Dr. Tony Evans's ministry philosophy as expressed through the kingdom agenda. Training courses focus on leadership development and discipleship in these five tracks:

- Bible and theology
- Personal growth
- Family and relationships
- Church health and leadership development
- Society and community impact strategies

The TETC program includes courses for both local and online students. Furthermore, TETC programming includes course work for non-student attendees. Pastors, Christian leaders, and Christian laity, both local and at a distance, can seek out the Kingdom Agenda Certificate for personal, spiritual, and professional development. For more information, visit tonyevanstraining.org.

Kingdom Agenda Pastors (KAP) provides a viable network for *like-minded pastors* who embrace the kingdom agenda philosophy. Pastors have the opportunity to go deeper with Dr. Tony Evans as they are given greater biblical knowledge, practical applications, and resources to impact individuals, families, churches, and communities. KAP welcomes *senior and associate pastors* of all churches. KAP also offers an annual summit held each year in Dallas with intensive seminars, workshops, and resources. For more information, visit kafellowship.org.

Pastors' Wives Ministry, founded by Dr. Lois Evans, provides *counsel, encouragement*, and *spiritual resources* for pastors' wives as they serve with their husbands in the ministry. A primary focus of the ministry is the KAP Summit that offers senior pastors' wives a safe place to *reflect, renew*, and *relax* along with training in personal development, spiritual growth, and care for their emotional and physical well-being. For more information, visit loisevans.org.

Kingdom Community Impact

The outreach programs of the Urban Alternative seek to provide positive impact to individuals, churches, families, and communities through a variety of ministries. We see these efforts as necessary to our calling as a ministry and essential to the communities we serve. With training on how to initiate and maintain programs to adopt schools, or provide homeless services, or partner toward unity and justice with the local police precincts, which creates a connection between the police and our community, we, as a ministry, live out God's kingdom agenda according to our Kingdom Strategy for Community Transformation.

The Kingdom Strategy for Community Transformation is a three-part plan that equips churches to have a positive impact on their communities for the kingdom of God. It also provides numerous practical suggestions for how this three-part plan can be implemented in your community, and it serves as a blueprint for unifying churches around the common goal of creating a better world for all of us. Visit tonyevans.org to access the three-part plan.

National Church Adopt-a-School Initiative (NCAASI) prepares churches across the country to impact communities by using *public schools as the primary vehicle for effecting positive social change* in urban youth and families. Leaders of churches, school districts, faith-based organizations, and other nonprofit organizations are equipped with the knowledge and tools to *forge partnerships* and build *strong social service delivery systems*. This training is based on the comprehensive church-based community impact strategy conducted by Oak Cliff Bible Fellowship. It addresses such areas as economic development, education, housing, health revitalization, family renewal, and racial reconciliation. We assist churches in tailoring the model to meet specific needs of their communities while simultaneously addressing the spiritual and moral frame of reference. Training events are held annually at Oak Cliff Bible Fellowship. For more information, visit churchadoptaschool.org.

Athlete's Impact (AI) exists as an outreach both into and through the sports arena. Coaches can be the most influential individuals in young people's lives, even ahead of their parents. With the growing rise of fatherlessness in our culture, more young people are looking to their coaches for guidance, character development, practical needs, and hope. After coaches on the influencer scale fall athletes. Athletes (whether professional or amateur) influence younger athletes and kids within their spheres of impact. Knowing this, we have made it our aim to equip and train coaches and athletes on how to live out and utilize their God-given roles for the benefit of the kingdom. We aim to do this through our iCoach App as well as resources such as *The Playbook: A Life Strategy Guide for Athletes*. For more information, visit icoachapp.org.

Tony Evans Films ushers in positive life change through compelling video shorts, animation, and feature-length films. We seek to build kingdom disciples through the power of story. We use a variety of platforms for viewer consumption and have had over 100 million digital views. We also merge video shorts and film with relevant Bible study materials to bring people to the saving knowledge of Jesus Christ and to strengthen the body of Christ worldwide. Tony Evans Films released its first feature-length film, *Kingdom Men Rising*, in April 2019 in over 800 theaters nationwide, in partnership with LifeWay Films. The second release, *Journey With Jesus*, is in partnership with RightNow Media.

Resource Development

We are fostering lifelong learning partnerships with the people we serve by providing a variety of published materials. Dr. Evans has published more than 125 unique titles based on over 50 years of preaching, including booklets, books, and Bible studies. He also holds the honor of writing and publishing the first full-Bible commentary and study Bible by an African American, which released in 2019. This Bible sits on permanent display as a historic release in The Museum of the Bible in Washington, DC.

For more information, and a complimentary copy of Dr. Evans' devotional newsletter, call (800) 800-3222, write to TUA at P.O. Box 4000, Dallas, TX 75208, or visit us online at www.tonyevans.org.

NOTES

Chapter One: Chosen for the Challenge

1. "The Legacy of a Man," Oak Cliff Bible Fellowship, accessed September 28, 2020, https://www.ocbfchurch.org/weekly -devotion/adam-where-you-at/the-legacy -of-a-man/.

2. Jonathan Adams, "Shaquem Griffin: 5 Fast Facts You Need to Know, " Heavy, March 3, 2018, https://heavy.com/sports /2018/03/shaquem-griffin-hand-how-loss -arm-why/.

3. Adams, "Shaquem Griffin."

4. As quoted in Adams, "Shaquem Griffin."

5. Barrett J. Brunsman, "P&G Kicks Off NFL Ad Campaign with One-Handed Player," *Cincinnati Business Courier*, September 11, 2018, https://www.bizjournals .com/cincinnati/news/2018/09/11/p-g -kicks-off-nfl-ad-campaign-with-one -handed.html.

6. Bob Condotta, "Analysis: Call to Shaquem Griffin Gives Seahawks' Draft One Indelible Moment," *Seattle Times*, April 28, 2018, https://www.seattletimes.com /sports/seahawks/analysis-call-to-shaq uem-griffin-gives-seahawks-draft-one-ind elible-moment/.

7. Kevin Bonsor, "How the NFL Draft Works," HowStuffWorks, accessed September 21, 2020, https://entertainment.howstuff works.com/nfl-draft4.htm.

8. "Shaquem Griffin Reacts to Being Drafted by the Seattle Seahawks | ESPN," video, April 28, 2018, https://www.youtube .com/watch?v=QSFmuI-DAK4.

9. "Shaquem Griffin Reacts," video.

10. "Kingdom Church," Tony Evans Training Center, accessed September 28, 2020, https://tonyevanstraining.org/courses /KC.

11. Frank Newport, "In U.S., Estimate of LGBT Population Rises to 4.5%," Gallup, May 22, 2018, https://news.gallup.com /poll/234863/estimate-lgbt-population-ri ses.aspx.

12. "In U.S., Decline of Christianity Continues at Rapid Pace," Pew Research Center, October 17, 2019, https://www .pewforum.org/2019/10/17/in-u-s-decline -of-christianity-continues-at-rapid-pace/.

Chapter Two: Dry Bones Can Dance

1. Burfict to Roethlisberger, January 9, 2016, AFC wildcard playoff; Steelers won 16–13. See Curt Popejoy, "Watch Vontaze Burfict Drive His Knee into Ben

Roethlisberger's Shoulder," SteelersWire, USAToday.com, January 2016, https://steelerswire.usatoday.com/2016/01/10/replay-shows-burficts-sack-of-roethlisberger-not-so-clean-after-all/.

2. As quoted in "Ryan Shazier Gets Injured | Monday Night Football," video, December 4, 2017, https://www.youtube.com/watch?v=1_a-l4a-qgw.

3. As quoted in "Steelers-Bengals Marred by Worrying Injuries on Brutal, Ugly Night for NFL," the Guardian, December 5, 2017, https://www.theguardian.com/sport/2017/dec/05/steelers-bengals-ryan-shazier-injury-nfl.

4. "Ryan Shazier Injury: What Happened to the Steelers LB and How's His Recovery Going," SBNation, updated September 9, 2020, https://www.sbnation.com/2018/1/14/16883184/ryan-shazier-inury-news-recovery-steelers.

5. Cassidy977, "Pittsburgh Steelers vs. Cincinnati Bengals: A Complete History of the Rivalry," November 23, 2019, Behind the Steel Curtain, SBNation, https://www.behindthesteelcurtain.com/2019/11/23/20965187/pittsburgh-steelers-vs-cincinnati-bengals-a-complete-history-of-the-rivalry-week-12-nfl-news.

6. Alaa Abdeldaiem, "Watch: Ryan Shazier Returns to Paul Brown Stadium One Year After Spinal Injury," Sports Illustrated, October 14, 2018, https://www.si.com/nfl/2018/10/14/ryan-shazier-walks-paul-brown-stadium-one-year-after-injury.

7. Aditi Kinkhabwala, "Steelers LB Ryan Shazier Embraces What Makes Him Different," NFL.com, August 17, 2016, https://www.nfl.com/news/steelers-lb-ryan-shazier-embraces-what-makes-him-different-0ap3000000686243.

8. Dan Gartland, "Mike Tomlin Says Ryan Shazier Is 'in Really Good Spirits,'" Sports Illustrated, December 5, 2017, https://www.si.com/nfl/2017/12/05/ryan-shazier-steelers-mike-tomlin-injury-update.

9. Abdeldaiem, "Ryan Shazier Returns."

10. Some of the material in the remainder of this chapter adapted from Tony Evans, America: Turning a Nation to God (Chicago: Moody, 2015), chapter 2. Used by permission.

Chapter Three: A Tale of Two Men

1. "Yamuna River," Water Database, accessed September 21, 2020, https://www.waterdatabase.com/rivers/yamuna-river/.

2. Chloe Farand, "Floods in India, Bangladesh and Nepal Kill 1,200 and Leave Millions Homeless," Independent, August 30, 2017, https://www.independent.co.uk/news/world/asia/india-floods-bangladesh-nepal-deaths-millions-homeless-latest-news-updates-a7919006.html.

3. "Lalita Park Still on Shaky Ground," Times of India, updated May 16, 2017, https://timesofindia.indiatimes.com/city/delhi/lalita-park-still-on-shaky-ground/articleshow/58689598.cms.

4. "Lalita Park," Times of India.

5. "Lalita Park," Times of India.

6. "Lalita Park," Times of India.

7. "Lalita Park," Times of India.

Chapter Four: The Secret to Success

1. Elizabeth Hudson, "Secession Fever, 87 Years Old, Is on the Rise in Texas Neighborhood," the Washington Post, November 23, 1990, https://www.washingtonpost.com/archive/politics/1990/11/23/secession-fever-87-years-old-is-on-the-rise-in-texas-neighborhood/c692b9ed-2bed-4fe6-8095-90b58032e2aa/.

2. Steve Pickett, "All-White Dallas Country Club Admits First Black Member," DFW CBS Local, February 14, 2014, https://dfw.cbslocal.com/2014/02/14/all-white-dallas-country-club-admits-first-black-member/.

3. Jared Staver, "How Does Speed Affect Car Accident Damages," Staver Legal Blog, accessed September 21, 2020, https://www.

chicagolawyer.com/speed-affect-car-accident-damages/.

4. "The Top 10 Causes of Death," World Health Organization, May 24, 2018, https://www.who.int/news-room/fact-sheets/detail/the-top-10-causes-of-death.

5. Nikola Djurkovic, "How Many People Die in Car Accidents?," April 17, 2020, PolicyAdvice, https://policyadvice.net/car-insurance/insights/how-many-people-die-in-car-accidents/.

6. Adapted from "Day 1," Kingdom Disciples: A 6-Day Reading Plan by Tony Evans, Bible.com, accessed September 29, 2020, https://www.bible.com/reading-plans/15939-kingdom-disciples-with-tony-evans/day/1.

Chapter Five: Get Up

1. Quote adapted from *Rocky V*, directed by John Avildsen, written by Silvester Stallone (1990; Los Angeles, CA: MGM, 2004), DVD.

2. *Rocky V*, DVD.

Chapter Six: Get Over

1. Some of the material in this chapter adapted from Tony Evans, *30 Days to Overcoming Addictive Behavior* (Eugene, OR: Harvest House, 2017) and from Tony Evans, *It's Not Too Late* (Eugene, OR: Harvest House, 2012), Introduction. Used by permission.

2. *The Tony Evans Bible Commentary* (Nashville, TN: Holman Bible Publishers, 2019), s.v. "freedom," 16.

3. *Strong's Concordance*, Greek G1097, s.v. "ginosko."

4. *Blue Letter Bible*, lexicon, Matthew 1:25, blueletterbible.org.

Chapter Seven: Get Going

1. Numbers 25:9.

Chapter Eight: Get Along

1. This section and the one that follows, "The Power of Unity," adapted from Tony Evans, *Oneness Embraced: Reconciliation, the Kingdom, and How We Are Stronger Together* (Chicago: Moody, 2015), chapter 2.

Chapter Nine: Setting the Stage

1. "Major Hurricane Harvey - August 25-29, 2017," National Weather Service, accessed September 21, 2020, https://www.weather.gov/crp/hurricane_harvey.

2. Eric S. Blake and David A. Zelinsky, *National Hurricane Center Tropical Cyclone Report: Hurricane Harvey*, May 9, 2018, https://www.nhc.noaa.gov/data/tcr/AL092017_Harvey.pdf.

3. Mark Fischetti, "Hurricane Harvey: Why Is It So Extreme?," *Scientific American*, August 28, 2017, https://www.scientificamerican.com/article/hurricane-harvey-why-is-it-so-extreme/.

4. Bekki Poelker, "Call in the Storm," the *Chicken Wire*, Chick-fil-A.com, August 31, 2017, https://thechickenwire.chick-fil-a.com/lifestyle/call-in-the-storm-how-a-houston-chick-fil-a-helped-in-a-hurricane-harvey-rescue.

5. Imagined conversation based on information from Eric Mandel, "Elderly Houston Couple Rescued by Call to Chick-fil-A," *Charlotte Business Journal*, Business Journals, August 31, 2017, https://www.bizjournals.com/charlotte/bizwomen/news/latest-news/2017/08/elderly-houston-couple-rescued-by-call-to-chick.html.

6. "#thelittlethings - The Story Behind Rising Above," Chickfila, video, November 13, 2019, https://www.youtube.com/watch?v=OzuB4v5sPC0&feature=emb_title.

7. "White Allergies? - Uncomfortable Conversations with a Black Man - Ep. 2 w/ Matthew McConaughey," Emmanuel Acho, video, June 10, 2020, https://www.youtube.com/watch?v=CwiY4i8xWIc.

8. The NAS Old Testament Hebrew Lexicon, "'akal," Bible Study Tools, https://www.biblestudytools.com/lexicons/hebrew/nas/akal.html.

Chapter Ten: Furthering the Future

1. For more reading on the topic of fatherhood, please see Dr. Tony Evans' book *Raising Kingdom Kids*, Focus on the Family Publishers.

Chapter Eleven: Identifying Key Influencers

1. Adam Kilgore, "Branching Out: Mapping the Roots, Influences and Origins of Every Active Head Coach," the *Washington Post*, October 12, 2018, https://www.washingtonpost.com/graphics/2018/sports/nfl-coaching-trees-connecting-every-active-coach/.

2. As quoted in Ian O'Connor, "Andy Reid's Super Bowl LIV Win Is the Capper on a Hall of Fame Career for Chiefs Coach," ESPN, February 2, 2020, https://www.espn.com/nfl/story/_/id/28621830/andy-reid-super-bowl-liv-win-capper-hall-fame-career-chiefs-coach.

3. As quoted in O'Connor, "Andy Reid's Super Bowl."

4. As quoted in O'Connor, "Andy Reid's Super Bowl."

5. Pete Grathoff, "Andy Reid Gave Patrick Mahomes a Kiss on the Cheek Before Final Series of Super Bowl," *Kansas City Star*, February 5, 2020, https://www.kansascity.com/sports/spt-columns-blogs/for-petes-sake/article239983253.html.

6. Pete Sweeney, "Andy Reid's Quote about Patrick Mahomes Tells You Everything You Need to Know about Super Bowl LIV," Arrowhead Pride, *SB Nation*, February 1, 2020, https://www.arrowheadpride.com/2020/2/1/21118102/andy-reids-quote-about-patrick-mahomes-tells-you-everything-you-need-to-know-about-super-bowl-liv.

Chapter Twelve: Starting the Transfer

1. Gary Belsky, "A Checkered Career," *Sports Illustrated*, December 28, 1992, https://vault.si.com/vault/1992/12/28/a-checkered-career-marion-tinsley-hasnt-met-the-man-or-machine-that-can-beat-him-at-his-game.

2. Alexis C. Madrigal, "How Checkers Was Solved," the *Atlantic*, July 19, 2017, https://www.theatlantic.com/technology/archive/2017/07/marion-tinsley-checkers/534111/.

3. "Checkers Solved," Science NetLinks, transcript, accessed September 21, 2020, http://sciencenetlinks.com/science-news/science-updates/checkers-solved/.

4. Dan Lewis, "Meet History's Best Checkers Player," *Now I Know*, July 11, 2017, https://nowiknow.com/meet-historys-best-checkers-player/.

5. Madrigal, "How Checkers Was Solved."

6. As quoted in Belsky, "Checkered Career."

7. As quoted in Madrigal, "How Checkers Was Solved."

8. As quoted in Madrigal, "How Checkers Was Solved."

9. Madrigal, "How Checkers Was Solved."

10. Madrigal, "How Checkers Was Solved."

11. Lisanne Renner (Orlando Sentinel), "You Know How to Play Checkers. But...," *Chicago Tribune*, May 14, 1985, https://www.chicagotribune.com/news/ct-xpm-1985-05-14-8501300238-story.html.

12. This section adapted from Tony Evans, *Raising Kingdom Kids: Giving Your Child a Living Faith* (Carol Stream, IL: Focus on the Family book published by Tyndale, 2014), chapter 11.

13. *Indiana Jones and the Last Crusade*, directed by Steven Spielberg, written by Jeffrey Boam and George Lucas (1989; Hollywood: Paramount, 2008), DVD.

ABOUT THE AUTHOR

Dr. Tony Evans is one of the country's most respected leaders in evangelical circles. He is a pastor, bestselling author, and frequent speaker at Bible conferences and seminars throughout the nation.

Dr. Evans has served as the senior pastor of Oak Cliff Bible Fellowship for over 40 years, witnessing it grow from ten people in 1976 to now over 10,000 congregants and over 100 ministries.

Dr. Evans also serves as president of the Urban Alternative, a national ministry that seeks to restore hope and transform lives through the proclamation and application of the Word of God. His daily radio broadcast, *The Alternative with Dr. Tony Evans,* can be heard on over 1,400 radio outlets throughout the United States and in more than 130 countries.

Dr. Evans holds the honor of writing and publishing the first full-Bible commentary and study Bible by an African American. The study Bible and commentary went on to sell more than 225,000 in the first year.

Dr. Evans is the former chaplain for the Dallas Cowboys and the Dallas Mavericks.

Through his local church and national ministry, Dr. Evans has set in motion a kingdom-agenda philosophy of ministry that teaches God's comprehensive rule over every area of life as demonstrated through the individual, the family, the church, and society.

Dr. Evans was married to Lois, his wife and ministry partner of over 50 years until Lois transitioned to glory in late 2019. They are the proud parents of four, grandparents of thirteen, and great-grandparents of three.

Printed in Great Britain
by Amazon

80771814R00139